Surviving
Military Sexual Trauma
(In My Own Words)

A Memoir

Michelle F. Capucci

ISBN: 1534809805

ISBN-13: 978-1534809802

THIS WORK IS DEDICATED TO

My dear friend Kathy Sutphen,

for being unwavering in her friendship,

for believing in me,

for understanding my pain,

and for never placing judgment.

AND TO

One of the best "Navigators" employed by AMVETS,

C.J. Dickerson

INTRODUCTION

Unless you live on another planet, you are more than aware of how women, in general, have been treated over time. Sadly, not much has changed — despite how much information is publicly available via the various news agencies, television, internet, social media, and so on.

From my perspective, it seems we have taken several steps backward when it comes to the topic of Military Sexual Trauma.

Those familiar with the Tailhook scandal will remember that this series of incidents brought to light a level of disrespect toward women serving in the Armed Services of the United States not previously seen.

How have we taken steps backward? Even today, many believe it is a mistake to bring this matter out into the open because it only makes matters worse.

Attitudes toward women worldwide leave a great deal to be desired. And in all fairness, it seems men are not exempt from sexual abuse while serving in the Armed Services. So what is the problem?

In my opinion it is a huge lack of education regarding the topic of Military Sexual Trauma.

Some folks believe that women should not be allowed to serve in the military because it causes morale problems, poses distractions, and/or that they just don't belong. Some folks believe that if you take women out of the equation, everything will be just ducky. My opinion on that train of thought: it leaves no room for accountability on the part of the aggressor(s).

What is the answer? It is not preventing women from serving their country! And it is not lowering standards to allow women to serve! As an aside, you must understand that women serving our country are under extreme pressure to succeed. We love this country, too!

Again, what is the answer? Education. Do you realize there is little to no understanding of the difference between sexual harassment vs. sexual assault/trauma? I find that to be astounding — but it is true.

No, it is not for the lack of trying to educate the masses. It is the lack of interest, and, I believe, a lack of holding those responsible for this behavior accountable.

While we have made some strides, it is not enough. Disrespectful behavior toward women in the military is thriving and continues to be ignored by many.

My hope in presenting this work is to let you know I understand your pain, frustration, humiliation, and fears. I also hope to offer you a level of comfort by making you aware that you are not alone on this journey. The best thing you can do to turn this terrible reality around is to listen to your inner-self, follow your heart, and rely on those you trust to help you heal.

And certainly, be aware of your surroundings at all times. Be very attentive as to whether or not you are in jeopardy when in a specific environment: clubs, apartment, work site, shopping malls, sporting events, etc.

Finally, you must educate those around you. If we sit quietly and do nothing to resolve this terrible issue, we are basically giving our silent approval.

Sexual harassment, sexual assault, sexual trauma, and attitudes surrounding these matters are age-old. I am not suggesting this will be easy to reverse, but we must try to change attitudes by educating those around us. Failure to do so only leads to defeat.

And there has been enough of that.

A VOID EXISTS

Did you hear me?

A desperate question met with silence.

It feels like being in a vacuum.

Did you hear me?

I said I was sexually assaulted.

Did you hear me?

The feeling that you are not being heard is disturbing, because being ignored is always an intentional act. It is a way of dismissing an unpleasant matter.

Military Sexual Trauma (MST) is one such unpleasant matter. It is a matter dismissed throughout the US Armed Services chain of command.

How do I know this?

Many incidences, officially acknowledged, prove that sexual assault within the armed forces is real. MST has been addressed in the media, and even by the top echelon on numerous occasions.

More to the point: I was a victim of sexual assault while serving on active duty in the United States Marine Corps.

As such, I can share information, experiences, and heartbreak.

If, like me, you are a victim of MST, may this book help you find the answer to the question I have been asking.

Did you hear me?

FINDING THE RIGHT PATH

To give you some perspective, I must tell you it has taken me 42 years to come face to face with the damage I suffered from MST. Seeking justice and finding inner peace has not been easy nor pleasant by any stretch of the imagination.

And yet, this was a path I was destined to walk. I walked it with dignity, and I walked it alone. I buried the truth of what I experienced for 42 years. Hindsight has taught me this burial was a poor decision. Shame and not being believed were the reasons I made it, but again: it was not a wise decision.

I hope sharing my experience proves helpful on the path you may be walking. Perhaps I can show you some short cuts along the way.

I hope you view this book as a guide to finding inner peace, realizing at long last you are validated.

How does that come about? One difficult step at a time.

A word of warning: do not attempt to walk this path alone. Believe it or not, want to or not, you will need a navigator to help you through this emotional roller coaster. No, this does not mean you must seek professional help or a sterile environment in an effort to restore your wholeness, although you might. Seek clinical help if it suits you, and know that you can find assistance through a myriad of Veterans organizations. Only a vet can relate to a vet.

The reality of what you will be taking on is pretty ugly. It comes with sadness, but also joy. You will gain new friends and lose old ones. In the end, this is about you.

Did you hear me?

To begin, I am going to take a step back in time and invite you to visit the past with me.

FEBRUARY 11, 1946

It is the day of my birth, and while I don't have specific recollections from this exact day in time, all is not lost.

Even as a young child I understood the value of being born into my particular family, and I was grateful. We were not wealthy by any stretch of the imagination. But as a child, I did not know we were poor. Why? Because we were rich in love and life, and in the lessons that lead to the greatest of inner rewards: self-esteem, pride, a belief in our worth as individuals, and a sense of the value of our accomplishments — a sense we were contributing to the world. These were the gifts of my parents.

Their love was strong. So strong in fact, that defying his

Italian Catholic family, my dad married my mom outside the church, which led to his excommunication.

My mom and dad, Michael and Lois, were young when they began having a family. Out of love they had us four, Lois Anne, me, Mickey, and Angie, in that order, each a year and a half apart. I don't know how my mother managed to stay sane. We were all so young. My parents, in a way, grew up with us. While I respected that they were my parents, I also felt I could talk to them as friends.

Our house was filled with laughter: our laughs and the laughs of the neighborhood kids, all of whom were welcome in our home at one time or another, sometimes all at once. And there was music, sweet music. As I look back, I realize that music filled my life. Through music I visited the depths of my soul. Within our family we not only had wonderful voices but played many different instruments. Guitar, banjo, piano, organ, drums, and spoons were all part of our family's repertoire.

If we were not entertaining ourselves then the radio or television was doing the work. We listened to Lawrence Welk, Mitch Miller, and the *Mickey Mouse Club*. The songs kept our toes tapping and the living-room rug rolled back. We even grew to adore the tenor voices of Enrico Caruso and Mario Lanza, whose voices my dad imitated with his fine tone and projection.

Think about this: the musical scales are comprised of eight notes. Within those eight notes are endless possibilities to create something that, as a fine poet once said, "has charms to soothe a savage breast."

Okay — so we are far more complicated than eight notes. But let's not shy away from our potential, even though it may seem overwhelming.

My siblings and I were raised to value good humor, a strong sense of moral responsibility, ethics, discipline, and integrity. Always respecting others was paramount in our home. Listening to Dad talk about WWII gave us a peek into what it would be like to serve our country. I am proud to say my dad, my brother, and I served with pride and honor.

As a matter of history, I was born in the state of Massachusetts but raised in Florida. How did that happen?

My Father was a veteran of the United States Army and was

wounded in WWII. The injury to his leg left him with poor circulation and so he was unable to cope with the cold temperatures of the north. Relocation was the suggested remedy for reducing his pain. I am told I was a colic baby and spent the first three months of my life in the hospital, which may have slowed our move to Florida but did not stop the inevitable.

Post-service, Dad worked in construction and Mom stayed home. I don't recall locking our doors or being afraid to walk to and from school. I do recall that, on occasion, we were spanked or told to stand in the corner with our faces to the wall. Even though I had to sit at the dinner table until all my vegetables had been eaten, I mostly remember what fun it was just going through the day being me.

Who was I then? A little girl riding her bike, going fishing with Dad, and being taught to cook by Mom. My family life in summary would be as follows: we actually liked each other, we celebrated birthdays, holidays, weddings, births, deaths, and the successes of our friends. We laughed and cried at the appropriate times and we grew to respect one another.

As a teenager, I was anxious to earn money. My brother and I had a paper route and I loved it. It gave me time to let my mind wander free. We also cut yards and I ironed clothes for our neighbors and babysat often.

Looking back, my desire to earn my own money arose with my awareness of our poverty. Wearing clothes that Mom made from the same material to dress us all alike bothered me, even though I understood the necessity. Wearing hand-me-downs was rough because schoolmates are not kind. Bullies and snobs existed then as they do today.

Going to school was mandatory — "no ifs, ands, or buts!" When I failed the seventh grade I learned I was not too smart to study.

The following year I became ill with scarlet fever, missed a semester of school, and as a result failed the eighth grade, too.

WHO HAS THE ANSWER?

Somewhere around the age of twelve or thirteen I was being hounded by a question begging to be answered: "Who is this Jesus?"

I had heard about him from my mom and dad, classmates, neighbors, and friends. But their explanations were still vague and left me wondering. With mom's help, I got my hands on a city bus schedule and began planning my trip to a Methodist church. There was no preference to my beginning with the Methodists other than they were nearby.

Bright and early Sunday morning I found myself dressed and ready to go to church in search of the answer to my question: "Who is this Jesus?"

Having never ridden a city bus before, I was very excited and couldn't wait to take in all of the sights along the way. The bus driver greeted me with a smile and took my bus fare. He asked where I wanted to get off and assured me I would not miss my stop. He instructed me to pull the cord above my head when I wanted to get off. This was very important according to him, and so I listened intently.

His appearance alone made me think this was the kind of job he was meant to be doing. A rotund man with snow white hair and electric blue eyes, he had command of the wheel and I was ready to get on with the trip. My attention was drawn to each passenger boarding the bus as he greeted them with a special smile and gentle laugh. Yes, I imagined he had spent some time in a Santa suit once or twice during his lifetime.

Arriving at my destination he gave me instructions as to where I needed to be and at what time for my return trip. I doubt customer service and concern exists like that anymore. If it does it is probably few and far between.

Walking into the church alone was a little frightening, as I knew nary a soul. I did, however, notice one of my classmates toward the end of the service and that gave me some comfort. Knowing I could talk with her at some point about the sermon and examine her thoughts about Jesus eased my concern. I came to find out she had not been listening to the sermon and was only in church because her mother made her.

On progressive Sundays, we sat next to one another on occasion, but this proved to be a mistake. While her mother was criticizing what everybody was wearing she was telling me to sit up straight!

I regret to say I was made to feel out of place by members of the congregation, as they seemed to judge my clothing. No, I wasn't dressed in rags, but they made me feel as though I was.

For approximately five years I continued to worship with the Methodists yet never felt connected. I even sang in the choir yet still felt unaccepted. I also found them to be extremely judgmental about their friends. Who drove what kind of car and how big were their houses, or whether or not they smoked or drank or went to a movie or a dance. Later in life, I would learn that the attitudes of this particular community were not typical of all Methodists, but at the time it seemed to me that they didn't really understand the message of love or the Ten Commandments.

In the mix were the evangelists, who came to bring their message of salvation in the hope of saving all us sinners. When they came I sat on the very back pew for one reason only. They didn't just deliver the sermon, they screamed it. Talking about an angry God and a vengeful God and yelling about hellfire and damnation, none of which appealed to me. I wanted to find the loving God I had heard about.

Not long after making my decision to seek Jesus elsewhere, I said goodbye to my friend the bus driver. To my surprise, I felt my heart break as we parted.

When I reached the age to drive it gave me the freedom to explore other congregations. With mom and dad's permission, I was allowed to borrow their car to get me to and from my next spiritual destination: the nearest Baptist church.

Sorry to say, the time spent with them was short lived. While I understand "feeling the spirit" is important, I just couldn't get into clapping my hands, stomping my feet, or shouting amen and hallelujah. Just too much activity I felt. And again I was hearing a message about hellfire and damnation. There had to be something greater than what I was experiencing.

Only the good Lord knows where I ended up next. Wherever it was, the congregants were speaking in tongues and laying on hands to heal the sick. To be honest with you, I was a little scared as it seemed somewhat demonic.

The Presbyterians became my new friends after visiting the Episcopalians, both groups often called break-away Catholics. Suddenly I was hearing messages of love, joy, and peace. God didn't seem to be angry all the time and I welcomed that notion. He was fair, just, and forgiving.

Without making an effort to attend Mass, I found myself in a Catholic church and had little to no understanding of what was going on. I did not understand Latin. Needless to say, that was a big disadvantage since the Mass was said in Latin at that time.

Was I close to finding the answer to my question? I must say I was closer, but still not satisfied that this was all there was. In fact, many years would pass before I found myself once again asking: "Who is this Jesus"?

I am compelled to say my feelings or opinions about various religions are not meant to be offensive. Instead they are only meant to share my experiences within those times and places. My opinions on the matter of religion are to be taken as presented to you: my experiences. Believing in a specific "ism" is wonderful and should be embraced and protected. Further, I am not a religious scholar and therefore do not judge what is endorsed by any specific sect. In truth, I respect everyone's right to choose how they worship.

MY EYES HAVE BEEN OPENED

Growing up in St. Petersburg, Florida, the beach was a big part of our lives. It was an inexpensive way to spend the day. Pier fishing, gathering shells, or just walking along the shoreline was all I needed to make me feel like I was part of it ALL.

On two occasions I came close to drowning. The first was at a boat marina where my family and neighbors had gathered for a cookout. Scanning the sea, I noticed one of my neighbors out in the water, and I decided I wanted to go where he was. Wading out, I suddenly stepped in a drop-off. The fear of being underwater while struggling to find the surface was so intense I blacked out. The last thing I remember seeing was my mother running toward me. She

20

pulled me back to shore, and nothing anyone could say or do could get me back in that water.

The second occasion of my near drowning occurred many years later. I had been dating a young man whom I had known for quite some time.

Standing on the shore and looking out into the water, we saw what seemed to be a sandbar. We decided to swim to it. I was not a strong swimmer, and once we arrived at our destination we realized there was no sandbar. It was an illusion caused by the angle of the sun's rays. I knew immediately that I was in trouble.

Attempting to get back to the beach, we found ourselves swimming against the current. What does one do in that situation? You are supposed to turn and swim with the current, which I did. My boyfriend seemed to be a much stronger swimmer, so he continued on his course. I, however, was soon alone and exhausted, with only ocean in every direction.

The experience ended with me being rescued by a fishing boat, and it is something I'll never forget. They threw the anchor line, but by then my body was cramping and I was afraid I was going to die. Panicking, I grabbed the anchor line before it hit the bottom and it pulled me under. Using the hand over hand system I made it up the rope to the surface and found air. The boat crew pulled me aboard and motored back to shore. To this day I still have a real fear of drowning. And no, I wouldn't say my date left me there to drown.

Speaking of dates: The boys and men I have dated (with the exception of one), were kind, understanding, generous, and had great senses of humor.

I recall my first true love being grilled by my dad: "Son, just exactly what are your intentions toward my daughter," he demanded.

There wasn't a hole too deep that I wouldn't have crawled into!

Periodically, dad would go the VA Hospital for a re-evaluation of the injury to his leg. Many times I would accompany him and was puzzled by what I felt when I was there.

Men and boys of various ages were at the hospital because they were broken: missing limbs, blind, deaf, or making the best of being in a wheelchair. I looked at them in awe. They were in a restricted state as a result defending our country. Better yet, because they were defending my country. I was raised with a strong sense of patriotism but this brought it all home.

I began looking at my dad differently — as a hero. On more than one occasion dad was elected as Post Commander of the American Legion in our community, and reflecting on what I had seen at the VA facility, I was even more certain my dad was seen as a hero not only to me but by others who knew him well. The most powerful feeling I came away with from the VA experience was the sense that: "I live in this country, too, and I want to defend her! This feeling would occupy a great deal of space in my mind and heart for a long time to come.

At this age, I found an outlet through sports. I just loved to win. I loved the competition. I loved the smell of the field, the night air, the aromas from the concession stand.

I also began expressing myself through painting, and of course, through music. Yes, I've always been a fan of the arts. Being in the spotlight never bothered me. In fact, if I had to describe myself within our family unit I would say I was the clown. This proved to be extremely important, for without having humor in my life, I would not be alive today.

Do I have a favorite memory from childhood? Yes, I do. I believe I was about five or six years old and it was Christmas Eve. Brace yourself for this: I heard Santa's sleigh land on the rooftop of our house! Don't even think about talking me out of what I know I heard — it ain't happening.

But I also vividly remember the following: while in the sixth grade my teacher asked us to write down what we wanted to do with our lives. I wrote: "I want to serve my country in the military."

With my mind made up, I soon became one heck of an excellent student out of fear a poor academic record might keep me from military service. Before finally graduating high school, I had already raised my hand to support and defend the Constitution of the United States," and thereby became the property of Uncle Sam.

My dad said: "If you want to go to college, we will find a way to pay for it."

Of course, I knew what that would do to my mom and dad relative to finances. So I told dad I was already sworn in and would be leaving for basic training in fifteen days. I would like to think the tears that welled up in his eyes were from a sense of pride in his daughter. Not long after me, my brother enlisted. Let me point out that this was the 1960s, and our country was torn apart by Vietnam. So while some were fleeing to Canada, Mickey and I were enlisting. I guess Mom and Dad taught us well.

I was twenty years old when I left home for recruit training, and I felt like I was stepping onto the yellow brick road. I felt I was on the path I was meant to walk — the path that revealed itself to me in the sixth grade.

Recruit training is recruit training, no matter which branch of the armed forces you serve. But thanks to the disciplined environment in which I was raised, I did not have any significant problems adjusting to the training methods.

After recruit training, I would received orders taking me across the country, so very far away from my family and all the things that were familiar to me. I had never been on a plane and I had never missed a family Christmas, and one day soon I would be doing just that.

Sadly, I would also be confronted with behaviors by others that would rattle my world. I would be introduced to mindsets that were alien to me. My excitement at beginning a new life would be tainted and I would not know how to cope. I would lose touch with who I believed I was.

The philosophy "boys will be boys and men will be men" would make me physically ill.

I am talking about Military Sexual Assault/Trauma.

I AM ON MY WAY

It is zero dark thirty and I am awaiting transportation to take me to the next phase of my enlistment: recruit training.

My home departure point was St. Petersburg, Florida. I traveled by bus with other enlistees to Jacksonville for further processing. Once there, we were given a series of tests to best identify which would be the most appropriate job, or Military Occupational Specialty (MOS), for each of us.

My scores reflected talents in the electrical and mechanical fields which — **you guessed it** — put me squarely behind an electric typewriter. How classic is that?

As the day progressed we found ourselves, once again, awaiting transportation. This time our destination was Parris Island. During our wait time for another bus, some of Uncle Sam's chosen few decided to leave. I guess they did not know that would make them AWOL. The military police (MP) were on site and immediately ordered everyone to line up against the wall for a head count. Being the only female present, I was not required to stand there and listen to the MPs yell as loudly as possible. I imagine my gender let them know I was present and accounted for.

After a long day of playing the hurry up and wait game, the men and I boarded the bus for Parris Island.

Being the only female on this government ride I chose to sit immediately behind the bus driver. That was a mistake. Each time he stopped the bus he would open the door and whisper to me: "If you want to get off, this is your chance."

My travel companions and I arrived at Parris Island in the wee hours of the morning. The fog was dense, making it difficult to identify anything outside the bus window. I could not tell you if there were trees, trucks, houses, or other vehicles out there because the fog was so thick. Had I wanted to leave the island I wouldn't have known where to start or in which direction to travel. Our surroundings, hidden by the fog, made this journey even more mysterious.

Here's a quick history lesson to help you understand where I was. Parris Island sits off the South Carolina coast between Charleston, South Carolina and Savannah, Georgia. It covers 78,000 acres consisting of land, water, and swamp. And while it is referred to by some as the vacation spot of the world, it truly is not.

I would like to take you with me through recruit training. Take stock of all your senses so as not to miss a thing. When we step off the bus we take a deep breath and smell the dampness in the air. The fog is so thick it muffles the night sounds, and there seems to be nothing around us. Pole lighting, obscured by the fog, makes it seem as though I am sleep walking. The smell of the swamp is overpowering, but I am not about to say: "What stinks?"

Don't quit now as we are just getting started.

Exiting the bus we are immediately greeted by a drill instructor (DI). "Welcome to the vacation spot of the world," he says. "You turn your backs that way," he orders, pointing to the male recruits. He then looks at me and says: "You turn your back this way. You no longer know each other." He then asks for my orders, but I have none to give him, because mine are bundled with the men's. I try to explain, but to no avail. The response I get is: "How can that be? You don't know them!"

This simple little matter would come back to haunt me.

So when I was taken to the 4th Recruit Training Battalion, which consisted of all female recruits, I arrived without orders. My attempts to explain this to even more drill instructors only made matters worse. I was kidded and ridiculed and accused of being "special" because my orders were with the men's. To be honest, I did not care at that point. It had been a very long day.

I think I finally got to bed around 4:15am and the sound of reveille came at 5:00am. It came at 5:00am that morning and each morning after for the next eight weeks.

Now officially in training, we recruits were greeted by all sorts of new verbs, nouns, and adjectives. For instance, I had no idea what a "bulkhead" was or what "scuttlebutt" meant. What in the heck was a "head" or a "deck," and what did "port" or "starboard" mean?

30

The next eight weeks were a flurry of activity. Most interesting for me was the fact that the DIs were still wondering about the location of my orders. A long story short: without orders, I could have requested to be sent home. Without orders, what were they to do with me? But had I requested to be sent home I would have missed the opportunity to earn the title of United States Marine. And we all know: "Once a Marine, Always a Marine."

Believe it or not, recruit training has approximately forty phases crammed into eight weeks. Imagine the logistics involved in planning and executing military training for over fifty people in each platoon. It was like a roller coaster ride.

Now don't panic. I will combine these phases as we progress.

Phase one: Arrival. See, we have already completed this phase by stepping off the bus and reporting to Recruit Battalion. Wasn't that easy?

Phase two: Uniform Issue. There will be several more before we receive all our gear. See, I am already combining some of the phases by clumping similar activities together.

In training, each event is hurry up and wait. Receiving your initial "issue" requires you to be in formation with all your fellow recruits at the same place, at the same time, for the same purpose. You are issued all necessary uniform items and sundries ranging from socks, shoes, toiletries, laundry detergent, and more. The deodorant of choice was Right Guard. Additional uniforms are given for physical training, cold weather, and hot weather. Coats, scarves, handbags, gloves, raincoats, and various hats and shoes for the appropriate occasion are dispensed.

My favorite of all these was the Lyle hose. What are they? I am glad you asked because I, too, did not know what they were. They are hose made of a heavy cotton fabric and come in assorted colors, none of which are attractive. Dark brown, muddy tan, or spicy mustard were the limited colors available. And no, you do not get to choose a color. I did not and still do not know the purpose of these hose. Were they of heavy fabric to ward off sand fleas and mosquitoes? No. The two things I do know about them: they were ugly and hot.

Another aspect of this process was going to the PX for items not included in the initial issue. While there, I decided to purchase a hair brush for the singular purpose of displaying it during locker box inspections. More on this later.

Phases three and four: Medical. We were all treated to quality time at a dentist office staffed by Naval personnel. We were also treated to a physical examination to check the acuity of our vision, hearing, and more. We stood in line yet again to receive whatever shots they felt were necessary. In single file, we moved through the line being shot in both arms simultaneously with a pressure gun. I am not certain which shot they administered to me, but it felt as though they blew my elbow and wrist off. Did I complain? Are you kidding me?

My worst experience up to this point in my life was the Marine Corps pelvic exam. I had been given a thorough physical several days before arriving on Parris Island by my family doctor. Apparently that was not acceptable. Once again, I found myself in a hurry up and wait line to have another thorough physical exam.

While standing in line we were told to disrobe and were given a sheet to cover ourselves. Experiencing my menstrual cycle only made this experience more invasive. Upon approaching a trash can I was told to dispose of my Kotex and continue moving forward. After completing the exam I was free to return to the barracks but was not given any feminine products to block the flow of my period. Obviously, my uniform was stained with blood by the time I reached the barracks. I advised my DI that it was necessary for me to wash my uniform. After sharing the circumstances with her she was sincerely aghast. I felt demoralized, humiliated, and angry. I had to put those emotions on hold, though, as Marines are trained to show no emotion.

Phase Five: Officer Interview. Each recruit sits down with her series officer to share information about her ambitions, goals, and what motivated her to enlist. At this point I revealed I joined the Marine Corps to become an X-Ray technician. She was quick to point out that the Marine Corps did not have any medical fields. So what were those photographs my recruiter showed me of women in white uniforms? Surprise! They were all Navy personnel.

By now you may be viewing these phases as mundane. Let me assure you these phases are anything but usual.

At the sound of reveille, each recruit wastes no time in getting to the foot of her bunk to answer roll call. Each morning I paused briefly, upon the advice of my dad, to check for critters in my shoes. I am here to testify that Parris Island has roaches big enough to carry a bunk bed away in the night. Half asleep and not being in the best of moods, recruits must face the start of the daily routine.

As platoon leader, it was my responsibility to take roll call and report to the appropriate DI. "All present or accounted for, ma'am." It was also my duty to report the good, the bad, and the ugly, whatever it might be. I would like to think being selected to act as platoon leader meant something special. But it just happened — no big earth shaking event. Sometime later I would serve as guidon bearer and I knew that particular job had some significant meaning. At least it did to me.

Standing before the drill instructor is not fun to begin with. But it's even worse when you've had no time to brush your teeth or use mouthwash before giving her the roll call report.

In one instance, in an effort to soften the reality of morning breath, I turned my head just a bit so as not to breathe right into her face. Unfortunately, I had to report that one of the recruits was not accounted for. The drill instructor leaned forward into my face and asked me to repeat what I had just reported. Being obedient, I did so, and repeated myself. This time, she had to deal with my morning breath because we were, literally, nose-to-nose. For purposes of self-preservation, she turned away in slow motion and quietly told me I was dismissed. I wish you could have seen her face.

Three days later that missing recruit was returned to the barracks by the MPs. She was covered in mud from head to toe, sporting cuts and bruises caused by flailing about in the swamp. We were told to "fall out" when they returned her so that we could see for ourselves the effects of wandering around in the swamp for any period of time. I wondered: did she know there were alligators out there demanding respect for their territory?

As we all know by now, every day started with the sound of reveille jolting us out of our sleep. Then came a rapid exit from the barracks to fall into platoon formation before we headed to chow. Because I had never been a morning person, this early to rise did not make me happy. I had no appetite. Who wants to eat before the rest of the world is awake?

Phase six: Chow. My first exposure to the mess hall was an entirely new adventure. We female recruits lined up on one side of the "hatch" and the male recruits lined up on the other. The women were told that "men are trees and we do not talk to trees." Hmm — if you say so.

Chow was pretty good most of the time. Or maybe it was just a matter of being so hungry after training. We would have eaten anything. I did see my lettuce move on my tray one day. Even that big green tomato worm hiding in my lettuce leaf looked good.

Following chow, the platoon marched to class. Here we spent numerous hours over the next eight weeks. How else were we to learn about Marine Corps history, the rank structure, or matters relating to nuclear, biological, and chemical (NBC) warfare?

During training, one particular song became our anthem: a Bobby Bare tune titled *I Want to Go Home.* And we sang it with gusto and plenty of volume. I found joy in just listening to fifty recruits sing together.

Learning how to become one of the "few and the proud" was

inspiring and challenging. I asked myself: what good would this experience have been had we not been challenged to achieve and succeed?

Of course, one of the most important things to learn at this point is to act as a unit, not as individuals. I have to say my platoon did extremely well. To be specific: we won drill competition! That is only possible if you have successfully performed as a unit. I am extremely proud to say I was appointed the guidon bearer at the onset of training. This meant I carried our platoon flag throughout drill competition.

Phase seven: Classifications. More tests to determine where a person excelled, helping to give each individual the proper assignment should they graduate and receive their orders. This process impressed me. It instilled faith that my fellow recruits would be performing at peak levels when necessary.

One day, without warning, we were loaded into cattle cars, given gas masks, and taken to the gas chambers. Upon arrival, everyone was marched into the chamber and told: "When asked, you will remove your mask and sound off with you name, rank, and service number as quickly as possible. Once the tear gas filled the chamber, the DI began asking me one question at a time, at a very slow tempo. My mask was off.

"What is your name? What is your rank? What is your service number? Who is the Senator of Florida? Can you sing the first verse of the *Marines' Hymn*? Can you sing the last verse of the *Marines' Hymn*?"

Was I having fun or what!

Truth be told, I was having a tad bit of fun with this whole thing. You see, my drill instructor was also required to remove her gas mask while asking me all those questions. I don't know why, but the tear gas did not bother me. That seemed to ruin her day. She was experiencing symptoms of tearing, frothing at the mouth, and gagging. But I was not. Trust me when I tell you the situation did not make her happy. She got within five inches of my face and told me: "Get out of my gas chamber!"

Yes, ma'am. Dare I say I don't think my drill instructor liked me?

When exiting the gas chambers we were told to run into the

wind and avoid rubbing our eyes. Problem was, there's is no wind on Parris Island during the summer months.

Returning to the barracks, the exposure to the gas finally began to bother me. Riding in the cattle car, I was packed in with fifty-plus recruits who had all just come from the gas chamber. The smell of tear gas permeated their clothing and it had nowhere to vent. Oddly enough, I was beginning to feel sorry for my drill instructor.

Not long after this phase of training, our DI came in and advised us that the following morning we would learn how to "drownproof." Drownproofing is a method for surviving water disasters.

Oh my God! The word "drown" was terrifying to me for reasons previously revealed. Oddly enough, she also ordered us all to roll our hair before the following day's event in the pool. I did not ask the question: "Why?" But I was thinking: "Why does our hair have to be rolled before jumping in the pool?" No matter what, the DI is always right. News flash, I had never rolled my hair — ever. So that became an issue. No rollers, no this, no that.

The next day, here we go again. Reveille, reveille,

reveille...everybody muster! And everybody to the pool! As I was boarding the cattle car, my DI stopped me and asked if I had rolled my hair. "No ma'am, I did not." I was prepared for the worst but she just told me not to worry about it. With that, I realized we had a good DI and a bad DI. Kind of like the good cop, bad cop scenario.

We arrived at the Olympic-size indoor pool to be taught how to drownproof. We were told that if at any point we feel the need to vomit, then we should do it. We were assured that there was enough chlorine in the pool to "kill a dog." I cannot tell you how good I felt when I heard those reassuring words.

Our instructor stationed recruits at both ends of the pool, classified as swimmers and non-swimmers, the latter being me. Our instructor was a male DI and his voice is powerful within the confines of the pool area. I was ordered to the deep end of the pool. Because I had never considered myself a strong swimmer, I truly was in fear for my life. I was convinced I was going to die.

Drownproofing involves a few different techniques. For example: with only the top-most portion of your head above water, you must stay perpendicular, or at the position of attention, until you need to take in air. You must stay in the pool while exercising this procedure for sixty minutes. Alternatively, you may float face down while dangling your arms until you feel the need to take in air. These survival techniques are guaranteed to save lives.

Okay, so I didn't die and was not sent home in a flag-draped casket. The next challenge was presented. They did not kill me the first go-round so here was their next attempt.

Before us was a diving platform a hundred feet high. We were to climb the ladder and jump in the pool using a specific technique that would prevent injury. Are you wondering why this was necessary? It simulates a situation in which one may have to abandon ship. It is to make you aware of a safe way to enter the water as a result of having to jump overboard. And, of course, that is when one's drownproof training kicks in. So now we were all supposed to feel really good about being able to float around in the ocean for days upon days. It seems that eventually one would become shark bait. All-in-all I guess that would be better than drowning.

And yes, we still have drama going on as time passes. Once again, roll call reveals another recruit with issues. This one has expressed her distaste for training by attempting suicide. She used the venetian blind cord in the squad bay, which is also our living area. I am not sure of this, but it seems to me she should have known the cord wasn't strong enough to achieve her goal.

We were approaching the halfway mark of training, and that meant more inspections. We were advised our locker boxes would be inspected and that we will have "junk on the bunk."

What is "junk on the bunk?" Each locker box provides a limited amount of space to house personal items. A "junk on the bunk" inspection is just that. Items from your locker box are displayed in a very specific fashion on your bunk.

Do you recall the hair brush I purchased for the purpose of displaying it at this particular moment? In my mind, all I had to do was remove this unused brush from its' case knowing it would be viewed as pristine and I would certainly pass inspection. The DI picked up the brush, put it in front of my face, and stated: "We have pigs on the farm cleaner than you. Does your mother know you are a pig?" I guess they had been exposed to my antics by others and were not falling for it.

Okay, let's prepare to graduate.

Boot camp is filled with inspection after inspection after inspection. Each inspection has an individual purpose. Ultimately, however, they all have an overarching purpose. They are used to measure the progression of your discipline and your ability to conform to general and specific processes. To simplify: Parris Island builds Marines. The purpose of most of the training is to tear you down and rebuild you. They want to know if you are going to break down during training. If that happens, then what could be expected of you in a combat zone? That's the goal. Weed out those who are not Marine material. Inspections are a means to track your progress during your stay at Parris Island. Yes, there is a tracking system used to monitor you. I call it the "chit" system. If you screw up, you may amass x-number of chits, kind of like a strike or a black mark on your record. The Corps will use these chits to set you back to a new platoon, extending your stay for another eight weeks of training, if you make it that long.

So the idea is not to collect chits. That may sound easy, but the Corps has got this process covered. If you don't get a chit for something, you are very lucky. Example: I received a chit for having a "kitten," aka a lint ball, in the corner pocket of my robe. Hello? I didn't have a pocket on my robe. Now I had no intention of discussing that fact with my DI, as it would have been tantamount to cutting my own throat. Not getting into a "discussion" with a drill instructor is also part of training. Just say: "Yes ma'am," and let it go.

I received a second chit for ironing my towels, an activity that was strictly forbidden. Who is kidding whom? There was only enough time in the day to do what was absolutely necessary, and that did not include ironing towels. Instead, my technique was to remove my towels immediately from the drying racks, fold them as instructed, and drape them at the end of my bunk frame. This made them appear as though they were ironed. Again, I didn't suffer any ill-feelings about receiving a chit for this. I had washed and pressed my neighbors clothes and linens to earn money when I was growing up. But I was not interested in ironing my towels during recruit training.

When our DIs felt we were ready, we began drilling in formation. I don't know how the DIs ever survived this phase. We, as recruits, not only had to be alert and adept, but the DI had to be pretty damn good at teaching the art of drill and precision drilling for purposes of competition. We not only had female instructors but also male instructors involved in this training. Visually, the DI wanted it to seem as though 100 individuals were moving as one.

I am more than proud to say, our platoon won drill competition in the dead heat of summer at Parris Island. Sand fleas and all, we did it!

In recognition of this particular achievement, a formal ceremony was conducted.

Everybody who competed was now in company formation on the drill field preparing to be recognized. Winning drill competition meant we not only carried the pride of this achievement, but a streamer was tied to our platoon flag, carried by the guidon bearer, for everyone at the ceremony to see. As guidon bearer, it was a moment in time I shall never forget.

Are we past all the drama? No, we are not.

One recruit decided it was easier to douse herself with lighter fluid and strike a match rather than complete training. Don't ask me to explain her mindset. It was a puzzle to me. But even more disturbing events followed. While laying on the floor of the company office in a semi-fetal position, the unexpected happened. The DI approached her and delivered a kick to her ribs, telling her to: "Get up. You are not hurt."

I believe it is safe to say this recruit was processed for discharge. And more than likely it was not under honorable conditions.

About to graduate, we finally realized what it meant to be a senior platoon. We were afforded free time to spit shine our shoes or sit and enjoy the warmth of the sun. I chose the latter. We were also surprised by the news we were going on liberty.

My memory takes me back to Charleston, South Carolina, to watch the movie *Paint Your Wagon*. Even though we were on liberty, we were accompanied by our DI. We were also made aware that we'd be expected to sit at the position of attention throughout the movie. Did we have popcorn? Are you kidding? Some time later, on another liberty call, we were treated to dinner in Savannah, Georgia. Both of these events were a welcome reprieve from the rigors of training.

We had now completed all phases of training, including the

physical aspects of sit-ups leg lifts, push-ups, squat thrusts, and running any unknown number of laps.

I should mention that mail call was an all-important part of the day in two specific ways. It was either depressing or uplifting. Some did not receive mail from home.

Now there was only one thing left to do before graduating and that was pay call. Picking up my check and realizing I was now earning my way in the world was an exciting moment. My first expenditure would be to buy a bus ticket out of South Carolina. In all honesty, you never really leave Parris Island, as it remains a part of you always.

Graduation from boot camp was approaching and my parents were going to attend the ceremony. How wonderful was that? I have no words to adequately express what that meant to me. What another wonderful moment in my life.

We'd completed eight weeks of training and were looking forward to the graduation ceremonies. Several commands were heard loud and clear in preparation for the formal ceremony. The platoon was ordered to come to attention and pass in review. Hearing the words forward march let us know this was real. At that precise moment the Marine Band begins to play the *Marines' Hymn*. It was then that we all realized we were now part of an elite group that would stand the test of time.

Upon graduating, I was looking forward to orders that would take me to my first duty station. I thought I was on my way, but not so fast. I learned I would be spending another four weeks at Parris Island attending Personnel Administration School.

The transition between recruit training and PA school was awkward. One day you're not supposed to breathe unless the DI says it is okay. The next day you're trying to find balance in a new environment of freedom.

GO WEST

Following PA school, I now had my orders in hand. It was quite surprising and very exciting. I was ordered to report to the Marine Corps Recruit Depot in San Diego, California, on December 16th, 1966. These orders would take me three thousand miles away from my family. They would force me to face my first Christmas away from those I loved dearly.

Reporting to my duty station in San Diego at that time of year gave me an interesting introduction to life away from home during the holidays. I don't think there were six people in the squad bay during that time. Because I was new and did not know anyone, I closed my eyes and imagined Christmas at home — not in a sad way, but with serenity.

Each holiday after that, I would volunteer to stand duty to allow those living afar to take leave and spend the holidays with their families. While I was standing duty, someone in the barracks would volunteer to bring me chow from the mess hall. Honestly, holiday chow from the mess hall was great. Ham, turkey, mashed potatoes, corn, beans, and all the rest of the traditional trimmings.

After each holiday, I would receive photo's depicting my family's holiday gathering. How I enjoyed looking at their smiling faces standing over a twenty-two pound turkey. Even the dog was smiling in anticipation of receiving a morsel.

My first assignment was to provide administrative support in motor transport. Ninety-six men and little ol' me made up the motor pool compliment.

I know it is difficult to believe, but these young men became my "big brothers." About suitors, they told me who I should or should not date, what company they should be assigned to, and what time I should be back at the barracks. I was so thankful for each and every one of them. Their mothers should have been proud of their sons and of themselves. Those moms were very successful in teaching their sons to respect women.

Someone told me the base was forming a women's volleyball team. With my love of sports, I could not pass up this opportunity.

Playing volleyball for the Marine Corps Recruit Depot in San Diego was too good to be true. Yes, I tried out for the team, and yes, I made the first string. Our coach was Hawaiian and what a talent he was. Coaching females was not an issue for him. He wanted that volleyball championship. He inspired us by telling us he knew what we were capable of and that we should believe in ourselves.

He drilled into our heads that no ball should ever touch the ground. We practiced in long sleeved sweats so that the material would be there to provide protection should it become necessary for us to slide to return a spiked ball. Not wanting to fail his leadership and belief in us as a winning team we gave him our all.

It is tournament day! We are playing with a full roster and we are ready to win.

We are not only playing against another team, but against other branches of the service. For those of you who do not know — a round robin is a specific number of wins and losses that either advances a team or eliminates a team competing for the championship.

We played with sprains, broken and dislocated fingers, and injuries that should have been enough to bring us to our knees. But in 1967 our volleyball team won the 11th Naval District Championship and I was glad I was a part of it all.

Thanks coach.

LETTERS AND NEWS FROM HOME

Where to begin? It seemed that suddenly everything was happening at the same time.

I received photos of my brother's wedding, and then they told me my youngest sister said "yes" to a marriage proposal. It just so happened she married my brother's best friend.

It seemed everything was going well for my family and I was excited about their joy. My siblings had begun their own lives and my brother was a soon-to-be father.

(Fast forwarding: he is still married to his one-and-only bride and has two children, a boy and a girl, and he has been a grandfather for many years. I believe my brother was born to be a grandfather.

He just melts when he is within arms' reach of a small child. Obviously, he has proven to be a loyal husband, father, and grandfather. I am so very proud of him.)

My youngest sister, like myself, did not have children. And no, I don't feel like I missed the boat regarding this issue. The endless hours of sitting for other people's children while growing up cured me from wanting children. Plus, I really don't have a strong stomach. If I were expected to change a diaper it would be a simple matter of no way! Let the kid change himself! Thank goodness the children I sat were past the diaper stage. But they were not past the throw a tantrum phase or the let's throw our food phase or the "no I won't" phase. Have you got the picture? As I said, I don't feel as though I missed the boat by not having children.

My oldest sister, however, was a real concern. The man she married was not only abusive, but introduced her to drugs. She became pregnant and was in jeopardy of losing custody of her boy to Social Services. So when he was six months old my parents adopted him.

There did not seem to be an answer to the question: "How

do we help her?" Before my enlistment, she'd begun showing signs of serious mood swings, but was having no part of counseling.

Over the years she has snorted, sniffed, and shot up anything and everything she could get her hands on. When I last saw her she no longer had that beautiful singing voice. The cartilage in her nose was deteriorating from whatever it was she was inhaling. She and her husband finally divorced but she still refused help. The lesson here is that abusers of anything have to want to help themselves.

Needless to say, over time this had taken a tremendous toll on our family. In the early days, it also affected my military service.

Yes, I have a sister who is a drug addict and an alcoholic. Her behavior was given serious review when my background check was being investigated for a Top Secret clearance. In terms of my service, her addiction would eventually have an even more significant effect. Eventually, her behavior would cause me to give up my career. More on that later.

Sadly, my sister paid the price of her addiction by having her freedom take away. She became a ward of the state. She had only one problem as I see it: how do I get my next fix?

For many years she was in and out of the penal system serving varying lengths of sentences. Nothing seemed to impact the more sensible side of her judgment. Over the years she has broken many laws, hurt many people, and to this day cannot seem to get her life back together. I guess that's what addiction does to people.

I spoke to her one day about all this and her response was: "I am only hurting myself." How crazy is that? I don't care if you are succeeding or are failing, you do affect those around you. Whether it is family, friends, neighbors, teachers, or even pets — what you do affects others.

Who do I blame for her woes? My family? Her schoolmates? neighbors? Social Services? the court system for not offering rehab? None of the above. I blame her.

All combined, I think she spent fifteen to seventeen years in jail and prison.

As for my folks, I thought all this would kill both of them. The drama was extreme and caused friction between them on a daily basis. Finally exercising tough love, they stopped rescuing her. And that was the best thing they could have done for themselves. Yeah,

Mom and Dad!

Several years after my mom died my sister called to tell me she did not know that her addiction was an illness and she apologized for hurting me. She was in her early 50s when she made that discovery. She volunteered that she was in rehab and was proud of her progress. I have to say, I was pretty pissed with her attitude. As I'll explain, she cost me my career — but she is proud of her progress in rehab? Give me a break!

However, in one of my more rational moments, I began to re-evaluate my anger and came to realize two truths. One: at least she finally took pro-active steps to try and deal with her array of addictions. And two: she was not aware of my disdain. Therefore, I was only hurting myself by not releasing myself from all of this anger and pain. I was already burdened with my own personal pain because of my sexual assault.

For several years, I volunteered with at-risk-youth and found two serious problems. They are not held accountable for their bad behavior, and they are not rewarded for their good behavior.

In other words, behavior has it rewards and its consequences.

It is up to each of us to choose our **path**. And when it doesn't work

out — don't go pointing fingers.

I WISH I KNEW

Time does strange things to us all and I suppose it is meant to keep us on our toes, although don't take my word for it.

You may be wondering how my oldest sister is doing. Is she okay? Is she still in rehab? Is she involved in a meaningful relationship? Is she a kind person? Is she aware of the pain she has placed upon the doorstep of those with whom she shares the same bloodline? Or, has she failed in her efforts to remain clean?

Sometimes I wish I knew.

I haven't seen or heard from my older sister in many years. I believe, however, that this is for the best at this stage in our lives. Truly, there is a point when we must put ourselves first. And I believe I am a much stronger person as a result of my relationship with my sister.

While I empathized with my family I had to refocus and turn my attention to my duty assignment.

My military career was progressing and I was soon promoted.

As I mentioned earlier I was assigned to Motor Transport while stationed in San Diego. In that capacity I provided administrative support to the unit along with other miscellaneous duties. Part of my job required me to deliver mail to various locations on base. I was given a golf cart to use instead of a vehicle from the motor pool. I referred to this golf cart as my convertible

As a prelude to what I am about to share with you, I must give you some background information relative to military tradition.

Upon promotion, the higher ranking people you work with are expected to pin on your stripes. For good luck, your fellow marines are then given the opportunity to literally punch the rank being applied to your uniform sleeve. Keep in mind I worked with ninety-six men. Ouch!

The following day, on my mail route, I failed to signal a turn and was pulled over by an MP. I explained to him that I couldn't lift my arm to signal. He wasn't buying any of that until I rolled up my sleeve and showed him my bruises. He let me go without giving me a citation. Can you picture this: the MP in his truck and me in my golf cart. It was too funny.

Several months later I received orders to report to Pentagon Duty at Headquarters, US Marine Corps, in Arlington, Virginia. Wow! I was heading back east.

Almost immediately after reporting for duty at my new post in Virginia I was informed an error had been made. The billet (aka vacancy) at the Pentagon required a rank one step above mine. This made me ineligible to work there. So instead I was assigned to work for the Chief of Staff at HQMC at the Navy Annex in Arlington. My background check had been completed and I was granted a Top Secret clearance. Just to give you some feel for the importance of this assignment: the Chief of Staff is the third highest ranking officer in the Marine Corps.

My new job was very demanding and that made for some very long days. But I was doing what I loved. Serving my country was all I ever wanted and I was already being called a lifer, a term used when those around you believe you will serve a twenty year hitch. I worked with an all-male compliment of varying ages and rank. That gave us an interesting blend of experiences, which I welcomed. It was impossible not to learn from them.

Some of these men had already served one or two tours in Vietnam and were ready to go again if necessary. Leaving their families was a difficult thing to do, but it was all for a greater good. By protecting this country, they were protecting their families and others for whom they cared and loved.

My folks would call and ask about my day but, because of my Top Secret clearance, I had to respond by saying: "I can't talk about it." At the end of my day I was to remove my typewriter ribbon, shred it, place it in a burn bag and take it to the furnace. If I had to pick up classified material, I had to go to security, show my ID, and sign for the documents.

Every so often the folks in security would make the rounds to specific offices and change the combinations of the safes without warning. Not being able to access the safe the following day was a clue to contact security for the new code.

And security was of utmost importance. Vietnam was at its peak and life in Arlington and Washington D.C. was filled with protesters. I witnessed marches on the Pentagon, riots in the streets, and folks bathing in the Reflection Pool. Draft cards were still being burned and many were fleeing to Canada. It was such a sensitive time, we were advised not to wear our uniforms in public once we were off duty. Nor were we to wear them while using public transportation.

I began to notice a change in how people interacted with one another. Anger and fear seemed to dominate those protesting against the war. Opposing views were often met with violence. Raised voices, abusive language, unfounded insults, and a general disregard for common courtesy seemed the order of the day.

There also seemed to be a sense of urgency to live life. After all, one may die tomorrow. No, I don't think this was unique to the Vietnam War. What I found to be disturbing was an absence of sensitivity toward others. My personal experience came in the form of sexual assault. Perhaps it was a manifestation of the "I might die tomorrow" outlook.

ASSAULT

I did it again and I'll bet you didn't even notice. But then, why would you? or even better, how could you?

I am doing today what I have done for many, many years.

What have I done? I have totally ignored, dismissed, minimized, and buried the topic of assault.

Why wouldn't I? It is so much easier to give the matter no energy. To deal with it gives it life.

Let me draw your attention to the word "energy." It is defined as follows: 1. Force of expression or utterance; 2. Potential forces, inherent power, capacity for vigorous action, and so on.

When dealing with the reality of assault many highs and lows present themselves in varying disguises. It requires a great deal of energy to even begin to cope with the reality of the pain and suffering.

There were mornings when my eyes would blink quickly in an effort to focus from another restless night. It was then that I realized I must face another day of darkness and demons. Dear sweet Jesus, how much more of this could I take?

Crawling out of bed felt as though I had a ball and chain shackled to both ankles. How do I find the energy to get through this?

I'll tell you how. Once again, I tried to bury this matter. I ignored what my heart was feeling and shut out what my brain recognized as pain.

Would committing suicide be the solution?

Many family members, friends, and co-workers perceived me to be strong, independent, and whole. Although I said to my close friends: "I have a heart like a marshmallow and banana peel for a spine," my physical demeanor presented the opposite. As a result, I did not feel I could share the pain of being suicidal without being dismissed.

I considered several ways to achieve suicide but kept coming back to the same one.

Drowning would be quick if done correctly.

Having faced the possibility of drowning in the past, I believed I could do this in a way that would give me some dignity as I transitioned from this life to the next.

My mind set, all I had to do was be certain the needed elements were in place. I already knew the preferred body of water in which to give up my life. Its temperature would add to a quick death. Its swift current would take control of where my body would ultimately be recovered. So far, it seemed like the perfect plan.

What stopped me?

Divine Providence is the answer.

SOME GOOD NEWS

The year is 1968 and I have learned I am to be transferred from the Chief of Staff's Office to the Office of the Director of Women Marines. Relative to rank structure, she is the highest ranking female and I am honored to have been selected to work for her.

Having suffered sexual assault, I am looking forward to no longer working in an all male environment. The move to the Director's office will be staffed by all females and they are highly respected within the Marine Corps. I will be working with the Director of Women Marines, the Deputy Director of Women Marines, and the Sergeant Major of Women Marines.

Knowing and respecting the rank structure, I was extremely

proud to have been chosen for this assignment. Various assignments within the Director's office would ultimately become viewed as historical. I have come to realize I am a part of history in a very meaningful way.

After spending approximately seventeen months in grade as Corporal, I am to be promoted to Sergeant. And that, of course, means I shall be going through the "pinning on of stripes" custom once again. This time, however, it will not involve punches from ninety-six men. Yes, I was very proud.

I could tell you that my job in the Director's Office was also very demanding and I could tell you it was also necessary for me to keep my Top Secret clearance. But going into detail about my job is not the direction I want to follow at this point.

Instead, I am going to brag. As a point of interest, I have not bragged about me up until this moment. Why? Because back in the day these various assignments were merely that: just assignments.

February 13th, 1968 marked the Silver Anniversary of the Women Marines. In honor of this milestone, an anniversary waltz was written. Because of where I worked, I was involved in many of the plans directed at making this a wonderful event, but I was not expecting where it would lead me.

I was ordered to dance the waltz on the evening of the Women Marines Silver Anniversary celebration. Fighting that idea tooth and nail turned out to be a waste of my energy.

That evening, before the waltz was danced, my fellow Marines and I presented a uniform pageant of "period uniforms" to honor the 25th anniversary.

At the conclusion of the pageant, a Marine Bandsman, my dance partner, extended his hand and lead me to the dance floor where the waltz would be introduced for the first time. The trip from the platform to the dance floor seemed to take a lifetime.

To this day, I could not tell you what that music sounded like. I was just a tad bit nervous.

Following the anniversary celebration, the search for a cover for the official recording of this special waltz music began. Numerous photographs were taken but none were eye catching. My dance partner and I were taken to a multimillion dollar mansion for a photo shoot. We came up empty again on picking an appropriate photo for the cover. If nothing else, I fully enjoyed the day.

Finally, I was sent to D. C. with a combat artist to see what he could come up with. Bingo! Yes, the image he sketched of me is on the waltz music cover. As a result, I became "historical."

No, I am not through bragging. During my time in the service, positive images of women in the military were often used for promotional materials. I was asked to pose for several inter-service recruiting billboards. These endeavors led to some pretty impressive photographs being taken on the grounds of the Pentagon and elsewhere in Washington. Celebrating Armed Forces Day took me to Baltimore to model the female Dress Blue Uniform while being escorted by a male Marine in his Dress Blues.

By this time the Director of Women Marines was addressing me as "Miss Marine." What a wonderful compliment. I knew I was not only doing the uniform proud, but I was also well representing the Women Marines. Yes, I was complimented by the support I was receiving but I also felt stressed. While I was out doing photo ops, nobody was doing my work. I shared my concerns with my boss but she assured me it was not necessary to worry.

One day, while sitting at my desk going through the mail, my mouth flew wide open. I was holding in my hand an invitation from the White House to attend a ceremony presenting the Medal of Honor to a Marine I worked for in San Diego at the Motor Pool. Needless to say, I would not have missed this ceremony for anything.

Yes, that event led to another photo op, but this time it was in the White House. My picture was taken with President Johnson and Gunnery Sergeant Jimmie E. Howard, who is proudly wearing the Medal of Honor.

No, I am still not finished bragging. I truly do not brag very often so I am going to take advantage of this opportunity and hope I have a captive audience.

This one is truly a "biggie" in my eyes.

Once again, I found myself in the White House for the purpose of standing Color Guard while President Johnson signed a bill allowing women to become general officers. One of my most cherished items is the pen used by the president to sign this particular bill. It was given to me by the President of the United States commemorating this historic event. It is displayed in my home with other "I love me" stuff.

Recently, I submitted many of these items to the Archives and Special Collections Branch of the Library of the Marine Corps. Hopefully they will be recorded in history for all time. If that happens, does it make me a relic in my own time? Ugh!

I am aware that all of what I have just shared sounds glamorous but it proved to work against me.

Being called Miss Marine, in effect, set me apart from other Women Marines. Or at least it did in their minds. No matter where I went from this point forward, my reputation preceded me. Not wanting to be exceptional, I made it a point to prove I was just little ol' me.

Realizing some success from my efforts I stopped being concerned about what others were feeling and thinking. Bottom line was I did not seek fame. These assignments landed in my lap and I am thankful for the experiences.

However, without warning I began noticing changes in my behavior. Subtle changes that proved puzzling to me. I began withdrawing from social events and became suspicious of my surroundings. No, I was not doing drugs or alcohol! Feelings of being out of control began to frighten me because I couldn't pin point the problem.

Returning to my love of music, I joined a small band on the base. Periodically we would travel to Quantico to play at the dances and other special events. You are going to think I'm am crazy, but as a performer, a person must step outside of themselves in order to pick up the microphone to sing or do stand-up comedy or any other form of entertaining on stage. In other words, one becomes somebody else in order to effectively entertain.

Why is it important that you understand this? Because when I was entertaining, I was no longer suspicious of my surroundings or fearful of what I could not see or hear. Give this some time to sink in and I believe you will understand.

Look at it from a different perspective. Put yourself in a scenario where you are hosting a dinner party. And let's say you had a crisis occur at work earlier in the day. It is distracting you. When your doorbell rings you must now become the perfect hostess. If your work day woes don't disappear completely, at least they have taken second place. When I am on stage I am able to escape, just as you did, while entertaining your dinner guests.

More troublesome to me regarding my behavior was my apparent dislike for authority. How in the world could this be? What is happening to me? Let's face it I am in a world where respect for authority is a must.

The answer to those questions and others would one day astound me.

After being sexually assaulted I did not effectively deal with my emotions regarding the matter. I did not share my pain or fears with anyone. All of this stuffing of emotions would have a serious effect on me throughout my life. Oh yes, some folks would say to me: "What's up with you?" How could I answer their question? I didn't know

While I am trying to deal with that unknown of what was wrong with me, I took steps to deal with another unknown. I became curious about the Catholic Church. After several weeks of research and conferring with a priest, I prepared to take Catholic instructions in the hope it would lead me to the answer to the question I had asked long ago: "Who is this Jesus?"

Having not been raised Catholic, the priest and I had some pretty interesting exchanges of ideas. For instance: why must one sit behind a curtain in the confessional when your identity is already known? I don't get it. But with an open mind and open heart he listened to what I had to say about my wide range of disappointing experiences in churches prior to coming to Catholicism. I told him I did not believe it takes a "middle man," meaning priest, to say whether or not my sins had been forgiven. Thank God he was young enough to appreciate my opinion. I told him I knew in my heart, after praying sincerely, whether or not my sins had been forgiven. He even seemed a bit jealous of my relationship with God. He never said that to me, but I sensed his awe.

And so, after many months, I was baptized into the Catholic Church. I am driven to say the following: I understand the ideology behind baptizing infants, but obviously the infant has no idea of the commitment that is expected by performing this ritual. Please don't be insulted or offended by what I say because I am simply pointing out that at twenty-one years of age I was fully aware of the commitment I was making to God.

What was it that the Catholic Religion had to offer me that others could not? In a word: reverence. No, I am not talking about the decor, I am talking about a feeling that embraced me when I entered the Chapel. Beyond that, I respected the structured presentation of the Mass. And with great joy I heard God say to me as he tapped me on the shoulder: "I gotcha." Apparently, He had been looking for me as long and as hard as I had for Him.

At the point in time of my becoming Catholic there were movements within the church I thought were wonderful. They began looking at face-to-face confession if you opted to do so, and guitar Masses were being introduced. Knowing my love of music I felt thrilled by the prospect. I may be biased, but a guitar Mass lends new meaning to the scripture "make a joyful noise." And if you were sitting next to someone unable to carry a tune, that too gave new meaning to the words "joyful noise."

Back in the day it was not necessary to lock the doors to churches as no one was breaking in to steal artifacts. Knowing it to be a safe haven, I would find myself spending time at two beautifully designed cathedrals where I could talk to God about my joys, and whisper to Him about my fears.

There are some things that remind me of my stature; one is to stand by the ocean gazing at the horizon and the other is to sit in a cathedral with vaulted ceilings and stained glass windows. Each of these settings provides an opportunity to listen to God's reply to my prayers.

Who is this Jesus I have been searching for? He is my best friend, and he was patient enough to wait for me to find Him. And while I know he has never left my side, it has been difficult finding Him at times, but not because He was hiding. It was because I was not seeking.

Can I tell you how proud my dad was with the news of my baptism? Can I tell you about mom's joy. I don't think I can due to the lack of nouns, adjectives, and verbs in the English language.

Dad and I did talk about his excommunication from the church and he was convinced he was doomed to Hell. Based on what I knew of the Catholic Church, I shared with him how much it had changed in its dogma since he was forced from the church. For instance, some things that used to be a mortal sins were no longer considered such, and even a few saints had been removed from the calendar. I told him a lot had changed. I am pleased to say I believe I brought some peace of mind and heart to my dad after all of those years.

The Priest I took instruction from was, without a doubt, a holy man. When conducting the sacrament of Mass one could see an aura about him. His words seemed to be blessed by Almighty God in the most profound way. He'd received orders to Vietnam and would leave soon. I can't think of a better place for him to have been a Chaplain. I caught up with him many years later and he appeared older, seemed much wiser, but no less a man of God.

At his last Mass prior to leaving for Vietnam he spoke with humor and with some trepidation of his journey beyond Arlington, Virginia. Still, he spoke of Divine Providence and assured us it was the right path for doing God's work.

Many times I would call on Divine Providence to help me through some very troubling times.

WHERE TO FROM HERE?

Several of us enlistees have gathered around to witness an unbelievable event. Sitting around a black and white television with poor reception and not saying a word was very unusual.

Then the moment came that left us speechless and covered in goose bumps. The Apollo 11 spaceflight was about to realize a successful mission after many months of preparation.

Mike Collins, Buzz Aldren and Neil Armstrong had landed on the surface of the moon in a spot called Tranquility Base. The most powerful words I heard that evening: "The Eagle has landed".

I had always been fascinated by science so this had my full attention. My mind couldn't help but take a trip all its' own. I could picture future flights shuttling passengers to the moon and beyond. And I could imagine how it would be to discover life on another planet.

Not being a fan of science fiction in any shape or form, I was always struck by the fact that in TV and movies, aliens were always portrayed as a threatening force. It's no wonder, because in these stories we earthlings always greet them with guns blazing. It's how we lay out the welcome mat.

And while I believe there is life elsewhere in the universe, if one should come to visit me, I am opening a bottle of red wine and kicking my feet up in preparation for what they have to share. I am going to want to know it all. Where do you come from? How long did it take you to get here? What is your favorite food? What do you do other than bouncing around from planet to planet? Do you have a family? How do you communicate? Are there any real problems in the universe that we need to be concerned about? When will you come to visit me again?

After the success of the moon walk, we as a nation were asking: "Where to from here?"

Over the years the space program has enjoyed other successes and terrible tragedies. In my opinion, this nation should have continued to give the space program anything and everything it needed to continue to explore outer space and its effects on the human body.

Neil Armstrong walked on the moon in July, 1969. In September of that same year my initial enlistment contract expired. Where to from here? Do I re-enlist? Or do I begin life as a civilian?

When one is looking at transferring to another duty station or serving out their enlistment contract they are known as "short timers." I was getting so "short" I could have sky-dived off of a dime and landed safely. I tell you this to help you understand what my mind-set was at this point in my career.

I had an 8 ½ x 11 grid image of the Eagle, Globe, and Anchor on my desk. For those of you who are not aware, this is the Marine Corps Emblem. As the days ticked down, I would fill in one of those grids. I did that until I had to make a decision about my future.

I not only had to decide what was best for me, but also how

best to support my family as they dealt with increasingly more stressful matters involving my older sister.

Re-enlistment time is a journey unto itself. If the Corps wants to retain you it allows you some room for bargaining. I was hearing some very convincing feedback supporting the option to re-enlist, but I was still torn between the Corps and my family. Do I best support them by returning home? Or will I be more effective in helping them from afar? Do I cross the threshold or not? Where to from here?

I was down to about seven grids on the emblem and thought maybe I should investigate my bargaining power. I advised the "powers that be" that I would re-enlist if I received orders to Saigon. By-the-way, my initial enlistment was driven by my desire to go to Saigon.

It didn't take long for the detailer (the guy who keeps up with all of the open billets) to let me know there was not an open slot for me in Vietnam.

In a counter offer they offered the following orders: I could be stationed in Stuttgart, Germany, Rota, Spain or Okinawa, Japan.

Say What? I was complimented but not interested.

Tapping into my bargaining power I asked to be transferred back to San Diego if they wanted me to re-enlist. Not long after I spoke those words I was sworn in, with orders in my hands, to Marine Corps Recruit Depot, San Diego, California.

You have got to be thinking I was crazy not to accept those "exotic" orders. No, truly not.

Have you knowledge of the philosophy of Feng Shui? Briefly, it is the ancient art of placement within the universe. My placement in the universe is in the South West. What better place for me to be but in San Diego. Please don't misunderstand me. My heart and soul was my gauge in the universe long before I had heard of Feng Shui. I only mention this because it has proven to be true.

I informed my senior officer that I would re-enlist for another three year hitch. Raising my right hand to "support and defend" a second time actually held more meaning. I had a deeper sense of duty. Once again I had been given the opportunity to serve my country.

The answer to "Where to from here?" has once again been

revealed to me much like it was way back in the sixth grade.

Upon completing all the necessary paperwork regarding my re-enlistment, I submitted a request to take fifteen days leave before reporting for duty in San Diego.

Yes, I was going home to visit my family.

EXCITEMENT AND TREPIDATION

I had not been with my family for a long period of time and was feeling anxious about what to expect. I mused about how we had probably grown as adults, grown in our varied philosophies, likes and dislikes, and in our everyday views of the world? My family had never had a difficult time discussing most matters, so I was truly looking forward to the exchange of thoughts and ideas. Of course, we had opposing views on some issues but nothing too serious. My most surprising discovery was how each of us had indeed matured. It was all good.

After being home for a few days I surprised mom and dad with a large check for half the amount I was paid for re-enlisting. I looked at them and thought: for twenty years they provided food, shelter, and clothing for me. This was my way of saying: "Thank you and I love you very much." One would have thought I had given them the pot of gold at the end of the rainbow.

My time at home was filled with mixed emotions. It became very clear to me that we had all changed in many ways. No, nothing unusual, just normal growth of ideas and opinions. It was good to get to know each other again.

Within a week of being home I decided I wanted to drive back to California. So, dad and I went car shopping. Because I had not established credit anywhere, good ol' dad had to co-sign for the loan. I am certain he knew I would not let him down.

Having made the decision to drive across country my visit home was cut short to allow for travel time to the West coast.

Here comes the fun part. I took my little sister with me.

What a trip it was! My little sister was a lot of fun and had a great sense of humor. This journey became a life-long memory for both of us. Her only responsibility on this trek was to advise me of the next town, according to the map, that we would be reaching? She was truly bad with pronunciation so that left me to wonder where in the heck we were! Pronouncing the town name of Tucson proved to give us many years of laughter.

We finally arrived safely and I played tour guide to give her as much exposure to the West Coast as possible before the end of my leave. We both agreed it was God's country.

When my leave has ran out I said goodbye to my little sister as she boarded a plane back to Florida.

BACK TO WORK

Having gone home on leave and driven across country with my little sister, it was time for me to put on my uniform and get back to work.

One of the things that seemed to captivate me about the military was that one never knew what kind of assignment was on the horizon. Therefore, when I reported for duty I was anxious to know what my assignment was going to be. Another thing that proved captivating was how they just gave you an assignment and were comfortable you'd be competent in that capacity. That led me to think: "If they believe I can do this, then I am confident I shall succeed."

I was assigned to work for the Battalion Adjutant (again in an administrative support role) working with congressional correspondence.

When a Marine wrote home complaining about one thing or another, the parents would often become upset. Sometimes, these parents would go so far as to make their Congressman or Senator aware of the issue in an effort to resolve the matter. Further, it was not unusual for a Marine to directly contact their Congressman or Senator with a complaint.

All branches of the military have a chain of command that must be followed to ensure a disciplined command. Stepping outside the chain of command was not the preferred way to try and bring a resolution to problems.

This is where I came in. Working side-by-side with my Captain, he and I would read and review all messages from Congressmen or Senators related to these sorts of issues and decide how to proceed.

Writing to one's representative because one's M-16 jammed while in combat is no doubt a serious matter. Or making someone aware that your poncho had a hole in it and needed replacing was also a matter to be scrutinized.

From the time I received the congressional inquiry I was in a race against the clock. I had to respond within a 24-72 hour deadline. This made for a flurry of activity. Contacting various personnel for investigative purposes was not only vital in these matters, but very time consuming. Some of these issues were as simple as a report of an AWOL Marine, yet still it required the same energy to effectively send a return message.

Having been assigned previously to Headquarters Marine Corps, I already had a pretty good idea about some of these complaints. Especially, as it related to the failure of a weapon. The problem with the M-16 rifle was widely publicized at the time.

My new assignment gave me a further glimpse into what our fighting troops were going through. So you may think to yourself: Big deal, a hole in a poncho is nothing when compared to the Viet Cong.

But sitting at my desk or going home at the end of the day made me realize that I did not have to worry about staying dry in the jungles of Vietnam. I did not have to crawl through a rice paddy wondering if I would be killed at any moment. I did not have to be suspicious about people around me who spoke anything but English. And I did not have to worry about "friendly fire" in addition to hostile fire. Napalm and Agent Orange were not a threat to me.

What I did see as a threat to me was the profound division in our country regarding the Vietnam Conflict. The absence of patriotism or allegiance to our nation scared me. Why was it so difficult to support our troops in their efforts to protect the freedoms on which this country was founded?

I remember my dad talking about coming home from the war. The country not only thanked them for protecting us but did everything possible to help them rebuild their lives. Not so after Vietnam!

In my current assignment I was also looking back at my childhood trying to figure out why the country was polarized over patriotism during Vietnam.

I mentioned previously that my dad was wounded in WWII, badly enough to have the Veteran's Hospital recommend his leg be amputated. He declined the offer. And when I would accompany him to and from the VA for treatments or evaluations I was amazed by his demeanor toward the other veterans. They had an unspoken bond between one another. They felt the words when pledging allegiance to the American flag. I watched my dad tear up when he heard our *National Anthem* being played and I heard him swallow the lump in his throat when *Taps* was played.

Thinking about my fellow Marines in Vietnam and praying for their safety sometimes felt like I wasn't doing my part, wasn't doing enough. I was wrong because prayer is a very powerful weapon against our enemies.

I recall my dad would sometimes awaken from a dream, screaming in a very low pitched tone. It was guttural, and sounded painful. For years he would do this, but was unable to find a way to share the pain of his dream with us.

Finally, he shared it with my mother who in turn shared it with me. I in turn shall share it with you. I don't know all the specifics, but I can see why he had nightmares.

True story: at some point during his time in the war, my dad and his buddy stopped to rest. His buddy was leaning against a tree while dad went to take a leak. When **dad** came back, he approached his buddy from behind the tree and **nudge**d him on the shoulder to get him up and moving. His buddy's head rolled! He had been decapitated!

Today, a great deal of necessary attention is given to our wounded warriors but in a far different way. Those diagnosed with PTSD are perceived to be a threat instead of being in need of treatment. They have suffered injuries.

Growing up, I saw my **hero father** constantly serving his community in various ways. He was **an** inspiration to me. Knowing my dad and his family came to **this** country from Italy and were processed through Ellis Island, I learned that the only way my dad could earn his citizenship was to serve **this** country. But don't get me started on today's philosophy regarding illegal immigrants. My dad, as did many others, earned their citizenship the right way.

Overall I believe dad's influence in my life added a great deal of value to what was being taught in school. Saying the *Pledge of Allegiance,* singing the *National Anthem,* attending parades on the 4th of July, observing Memorial Day and Veterans Day were all a part of my life. Not because it was being taught in school, but because it was being taught at home by mom and dad. The best example I can offer you is this: being the sole surviving son, my brother could have requested to be excused from active service. He did the opposite. He enlisted. Yet another patriot existed in our family.

SIBLING RIVALRY

Yes, my brother enlisted in the Navy and I in the Marine Corps. And, yes, he and I had some fun times pinging on the other's branch of service and insisting ours was the only worth-while branch in which to serve. My dad was silent through all of this, but I am certain he was thinking the Army was the best of the branches.

I remember sneaking home one weekend to surprise my family. Coincidentally, my brother had the same idea. While sitting around the dining room table he stated: "I believe the Navy can drink the Marines under the table."

Yes, it was more like a challenge than anything else. Was I up to this? Well, of course!

We were both asleep by 2:00am, but my wake-up time was at 4:00am to catch a return flight to Washington. I was so hung over from meeting my brothers' challenge I prayed to die so that I might feel better. I swear I could hear my hair growing and just wanted to shave my tongue. Later I learned that he'd gotten ill from drinking so much. That's all I needed to hear to convince myself the Navy did not drink the Marines under the table. "From the Halls of Montezuma..."

It was all good, wholesome, sibling rivalry.

A COMPASS NEEDLE

I must say bouncing from coast to coast at times made me feel as though I was a faulty needle on a compass. Finding "Magnetic North" became a challenge. It felt like being on a quest to belong somewhere. I wondered if a committed, meaningful relationship was something I was missing. I wanted to trust but lacked the courage to get involved. I was afraid.

Back to my West Coast assignment, some of the guys (officers and enlisted men) I had been stationed with in Arlington were now on their way to Vietnam and our paths crossed again.

On my off time, I was singing at an upscale piano bar in La Jolla, California. These guys would show up and provide me with my own cheering section. Over the next few days they would be heading to San Francisco and then to Vietnam.

How many would return alive, I didn't know. But I knew this: the first week or two "in-country" gave us a high casualty rate, as did the week or two prior to rotating back to CONUS (Continental United States. I didn't want to look at these guys and wonder who would be coming home alive.

It was around this time when one could make a donation and receive a bracelet identifying a POW or a soldier classified as MIA. I, of course, made a donation and received the bracelet identifying a soldier in the Army. In the late 1990's, I visited the Vietnam War Memorial for the first time. I found his name on the wall, laid the bracelet on the ground below his name, and wept like a baby. We don't have to know personally those who have served and defended us, we must simply appreciate their sacrifices.

Did I know working in this assignment and in this capacity would draw these emotions from me? I had no idea. But I believe it was what I was meant to be doing.

READY, WILLING, AND ABLE

I have shared with you my involvement in various photo ops and activities promoting women in the military while stationed in Arlington.

Well guess what? Once again I am being called on to assist in hosting the Joint Civilian Orientation Conference (JCOC) in San Diego, California. I must admit the armed services combined are pretty impressive. I truly am a witness to their capabilities and their dedication to duty.

JCOC participants make up some of this Nations' wealthiest individuals. Whether they are representing their individual interests, lobby groups, or simply promoting good will in support of our military personnel, they are true friends to those in the service.

This particular conference was held at the Hotel Del Coronado in 1970. FYI, even though this event was "kicked off" in Coronado, it would not stop there. The participants would be escorted from one military installation to another all across this nation. The purpose of the event was to raise money to make certain our POW's received mail and packages from home.

Having said that let me back up a bit.

Various branches of the armed forces alternate hosting the big event and this particular one was being hosted by the United States Air Force. Because the Air Force was hosting all other co-hosts were broken down into "flights" within which our civilian guests would be assigned. My assignment was to work the week-end only to ensure our flight members were registered to attend and all of their paper work was in order.

After the week-end registration I was prepared to return to my command to resume my regular job duties. Upon arriving back at the company, I had received word my Company Officer wanted to see me. Usually that is not a good sign. However, this time was different. She advised me I was to return to the Hotel Del Coronado for the duration of the JCOC conference. Well, somebody had to do it. Seriously, I was extremely complimented. She had apparently received a call from Admiral McCain requesting my presence throughout this event.

An opening banquet, business as usual in between, and a closing banquet was all I expected. I could not have been more mistaken. We were there to impress these gentlemen and we did so in fine fashion. One of the events required taking our guests to an air craft carrier to afford the Navy and Marine Corps an opportunity to show off their skills. I arrived on the carrier, via helicopter, after a twenty minute flight from San Diego. From that point on all I had to do was enjoy the show and thank God these men were willing to risk everything. Night landings, sky diving out of helicopters, frog men being scooped from the ocean, and exploding unused ordinances were all a part of the day's events.

Within hours of returning to the hotel my "flight crew" of donors was to meet in the room I had been assigned for the purpose of writing a check in support of our mission: to ensure our POWs received mail and packages from home. I have never been so impressed. These men did not have to think about giving, they just wanted to know how much.

Time had flown and the closing banquet was right in our faces. Did I need my dress blues? No. This was a black after-five-gown kind of banquet.

At the end of the event, my flight crew offered me jobs anywhere and anytime. They also wrote letters of commendation thanking me for my support and professionalism. These letters were sent to the attention of my Company Officer.

I was once again called into my CO'S office so that she could present the letters of commendation to me. Upon presenting these wonderful, meaningful letters to me, I could not believe what she said: "Did you sleep with them all?"

Yes, I took the high road and kept my mouth shut.

In July 1970, I received a letter from the San Diego Chamber of Commerce wanting to present me with an Armed Forces Community Award citing good citizenship, outstanding leadership, and exemplary performance of duty. I don't know if my CO recovered from that bit of news.

I must say in all honesty, that as good as all of this sounds, I missed my desk and looked forward to getting back to work.

IT'S JUST NOT FAIR

The following year brought more upsetting news regarding my older sister. When talking with my folks, they both sounded exhausted and spent emotionally. My sister would go missing for weeks at a time, driving my parents into a panic state about her safety. They had also received anonymous letters stating my sister had been mutilated and placed in the trunk of a car.

Fearing for the safety of my family, I made a very difficult decision. My career in the Marine Corps was about to end.

For the good of my family, I requested and was granted a hardship discharge under honorable conditions.

Some of you may be thinking my decision to leave the corps

was made in haste. Let me take a moment or two to add some clarity.

While the frequency of my sisters involvement with the law and the penal system had not changed much, the intensity of outside influences against my parents was extremely worrisome. They began receiving threats from unknown persons stating they would be harmed if they did not reveal the whereabouts of my sister.

I don't know if those threats were the result of drug deals gone bad or because of a failure to pawn certain items to pay off whomever, or if was just a matter of bullying my parents. Because I did not know for certain what the basis of the threats were I felt I had to assume the worst.

Because of my clearance I did not feel I could discuss this matter with my superiors for fear of how they would interpret the matter or how they would view its possible effects on my performance.

Needless to say there were a myriad of thoughts running through my head and my heart. I felt my career in the Corps was going extremely well, but I also could not dismiss what my parents were dealing with. I was torn.

With much trepidation, I finally discussed my concerns with my superior and began to move forward on my request for discharge. Within ten days my request had been approved. To make certain the information in my request was not compromised, I hand-carried the request from California to Arlington (Headquarters Marine Corps), where I handed it to the proper authority and witnessed them placing it in a safe and locking it. That simple act gave me a sense of security but also forced me to recognize the seriousness of my decision.

Looking back I can say with certainty I made the correct decision. Had I made any other decision I don't believe I would have liked myself.

Upon being granted my discharge, my co-workers (Marines) and I were involved in a ceremony in the Colonel's office in which I was presented a Certificate of Commendation and a pen desk-set that displayed the Marine Corps Emblem and reflected my dates of service. I shall never forget the respect and caring they showed me that day. And, yes, I still have the desk-set.

WHAT HAVE I DONE?

Fortunately, I guess, I started to pack my household goods to relocate to Florida. This gave me time to really consider what I was doing. I came to the conclusion that I would be a stronger support system for my folks if it was from afar. I made the decision to stay right where I was, knowing I could and would be available to them when necessary.

Packing for the trip I didn't take brought to mind a couple of things. Number one: you can never go home. And Number two: one can be too close to the forest to see the trees. The second of these two thoughts helped me forgive myself for not going home. Did I feel guilty? For some time, yes I did. But I knew in the long-term it was the only decision I could have made. It was a great relief to hear

my folks agreeing with my decision.

Mom and Dad, shown in a wedding photograph.

Home Sweet Home – short on square footage, but long on life's valuable lessons

Photo-op at Barnum & Bailey Circus taken in the early 1950's, with my siblings.

The December snowflakes fell no thicker than Santa letters at Claus Toyshops, Inc., North Pole, yesterday. With Dec. 25 hardly two sleighbell shakes distant, scores of children were sitting down to write that all - important letter to old St. Nick.

Santa radioed The Times yesterday that the most interesting letter he'd seen was from three sisters and a brother. So Florida State Theatres will treat them to a theatre party, and their parents too. A family pass good for one show at any Florida State Theatre will soon be mailed to them. Here's their letter:

Dear Santa Claus:

My name is Lois and I am 8 years old, I would like very much to have a Toni Doll and some clothes. I have been pretty good and I help my mother all I can. Next is one of my sisters.

I am Michelle. I am 6 years old and I would like a pretty doll also and a camera that you can look at pretty pictures, and if it isn't too much some clothes. Here is our brother:

I am Mickey. I am 4 years old and the only boy. I want a com-plete cowboy outfit, and the horse too, also a punching bag. That's all I can ask for right now, as my little sister wants her turn.

Santa, I am the last one, and my name is Angelina, I am 3 years old, and I want a baby doll and some shoes, and some wooden beads I can string, oh, and one more thing, some tinker toys for all of us.

We four will thank you very much and have something nice for you on Xmas also.

The Four Capuccis
2417 37th Street South

Santa wants the following children to know their letters have been received and carefully checked:

Richard Taylor, Ronnie Porter, Carol Jones, Eve Randall, Byron McIntosh, Richard Dowling, Bud Hale, Barbara Wachter, Terry Balara, Victor Anderson, Joan Dennison.

Also, Marguerite Lukas, Donna and Linda Nicks, Dianne Gilbert, James and Susan Kurtz, Norma Ashworth, Joe Williams, Linda Heinrichs, Harry Brooker, Barbara John, Jane and Gale Allen.

Our "Dear Santa" letters, in bold.

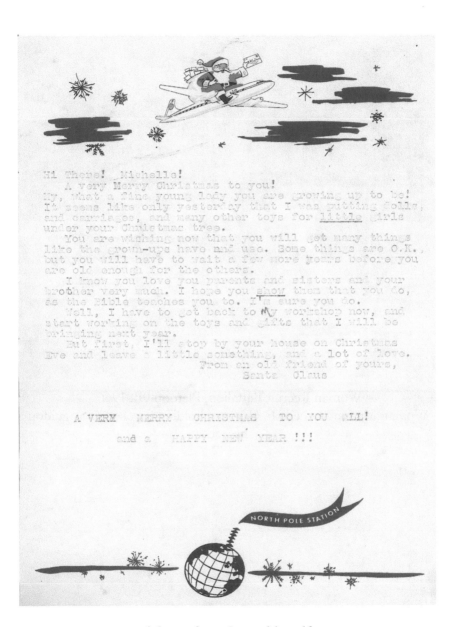

Hi There! Michelle!
A very Merry Christmas to you!
My, what a fine young lady you are growing up to be!
It seems like only yesterday that I was putting dolls,
and carriages, and many other toys for <u>little</u> girls
under your Christmas tree.
You are wishing now that you will get many things
like the grown-ups have and use. Some things are O.K.,
but you will have to wait a few more years before you
are old enough for the others.
I know you love you parents and sisters and your
brother very much. I hope you <u>show</u> them that you do,
as the Bible teaches you to. I'm sure you do.
Well, I have to get back to my workshop now, and
start working on the toys and gifts that I will be
bringing next year.
But first, I'll stop by your house on Christmas
Eve and leave a little something, and a lot of love.
                    From an old friend of yours,
                    Santa Claus

          A VERY MERRY CHRISTMAS TO YOU ALL!
          and a HAPPY NEW YEAR !!!

NORTH POLE STATION

A letter from Santa, himself.

Woman Recruit Battalion, Platoon 9B, 1966.
Woman Marine Michelle F. Capucci, holding flag, serves as guidon bearer.

The 11th Naval District Women Marines Volleyball Team, 1967.

Michelle F. Capucci

PAST TO PRESENT — At the 25th anniversary celebration of the Women Marines at Andrews Air Force Base NCO Club, these nine Company "D" Marines modeled the uniforms worn by Women Marines for the past quarter century. The Women Marines are (l-r): Cpl Michelle Capucci, LCpl's Mary Kay Mortell, Judy Grant, Myra Newcomb, and Wendy Moy, PFC's Karen Lindquist and Mary Vaughan, LCpl Pat Taglione and Cpl Kathleen Hanneken. (Photo by SSgt Zane Wilson)

The 25th Anniversary of Women Marines Uniform Pageant, 1968.
Cpl. Michelle F. Capucci, far left.

Cover of the Women Marines' Waltz Music, featuring the image of
Cpl. Michelle F. Capucci.

Colonel Barbara J. Bishop, who addressed Cpl. Capucci as "Miss Marine."

Marine Corps recruiting photo of Corporal Michelle F. Capucci taken
on the east lawn of the Pentagon, 1968.

President Lyndon B. Johnson signing a bill allowing women to
become general officers, 1968. Sgt. Michelle F. Capucci stands color
guard with the Marine Corps flag, far left.

Cpl. Michelle F. Capucci being greeted by President Johnson at a 1968 Medal of Honor Ceremony for Gunnery Sergeant Howard, for whom she worked while stationed in San Diego.

Cpl. Michelle F. Capucci being greeted by President Johnson in observance of the Women Marines 25th Anniversary, 1968.

OFF-DUTY DEPUTY CHARGED IN KENNETH CITY KILLING

A 24-year-old divorcee was shot to death early Sunday morning in the parking lot of a Kenneth City apartment complex and an off-duty deputy sheriff was charged with first degree murder.

The victim, shot through the head with a .38 caliber pistol, was Angie Margaret Capucci, who had resumed her maiden name after returning to live with her parents at 2417-37th St. S. following dissolution of her marriage.

The deputy, now suspended from duty and held without bond in County Jail, is Richard Robbins, 9, of 1706-Canterbury Drive, Largo, a veteran of eight years with the sheriff's department.

When police arrived he was unconscious from a scalp wound by a .38 caliber bullet, and was found lying alongside the dead woman near an automobile. He was treated at St. Petersburg General

Hospital and then taken to jail.

Kenneth City police were called by residents of Briar Hill Apartments at 5360-54th Ave. N. shortly before 2:30 a. m. Sunday, and Patrolman James Wright responded.

Upon discovering that the shooting was fatal and involved a deputy sheriff, the officer notified Chief Ruel Webster, who directed that the case be turned over to the sheriff's department.

A statement issued later by Sheriff Don Genung gave few details and said his department would have nothing more to say to avoid prejudicial pre-trial publicity.

The sheriff said Robbins, who is married, apparently was involved in "some kind of a domestic situation -- one that resulted in an unfortunate

(Continued to Page 4)

Clippings.

DEPUTY KILLS YOUNG WOMAN

(Continued from Page 1)

incident."

He said, "there were witnesses to the situation," but did not elaborate.

The POST learned the couple had been visiting friends in an apartment prior to the shooting.

Genung said the investigation by his department was in the charge of Detectives Frank Holloway and Don Shields, along with Assistant State Attorney George Osborne.

Genung said Robbins had received a "routine transfer" recently to the uniformed patrol division after serving with the criminal investigation division specializing in auto thefts.

Mrs. Capucci, a native of St. Petersburg, had been employed as a medical assistant in the Suncoast Medical Clinic.

She is survived by her parents, Mr. and Mrs. Michael Capucci, two brothers and two sisters.

Michelle F. Capucci

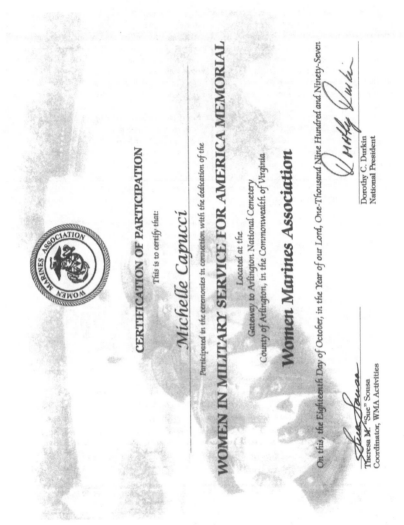

Certificate Of Participation: Women In Military Service For America
Memorial, presented to Michelle F. Capucci, 1997.

Photo and uniform display within the Women In Military Service
For America Memorial.

Front-page Chesapeake Clipper article, 1997, highlighting the
Military Women's Memorial and offering an in-depth look at Sgt.
Capucci's service to her country and more.

Sgt. Capucci, pictured above with flag in the Women's Memorial
2014 Special Edition Calendar.

WHAT'S UP WITH THIS?

My re-entry into the civilian world was not very welcoming. It seems my military experience was not viewed favorably as it related to employment applications. I have yet to see the logic behind that particular mindset. Administrative skills should be acceptable in any business forum.

For eight months I remained unemployed. That in itself is pretty scary when considering my car payment exceeded my unemployment check. I recall one trip to the unemployment office in which a young man who looked like a preacher's son said: "And what have we done to find work?" His words went through my veins like a wild fire. I told him I had done everything with the exception of selling my body. And yes, I was polite to him.

If you have ever been unemployed you are probably aware of the following: within a two-week period without a job one's self-esteem no longer exists. I didn't just make that up. That is a fact. I asked myself more than once: "What have I done?"

Feeling bad about yourself creates another set of obstacles in addition to the already difficult task of trying to find meaningful employment. You have to find a way to put a smile on your face during an interview while believing you will receive another rejection letter.

Eight months later I finally found employment and ultimately began working as the Secretary to the Dean of Student Affairs at the University of San Diego. The personnel compliment consisted of the Dean of Student Affairs and three Associate Deans. My military experience prepared me well for that job. Isn't that an ironic scenario to consider?

I must tell you the energy on campus in those days provided me with a new outlook on where we were in the world regarding respect, balance, new ideas, wholesome debates, and a host of visionary concepts. This was good.

Within the university campus was the School of Education, Law School, the Seminary and a couple of others I don't recall. But one thing in particular I do recall, as it was quite memorable.

Jane Fonda was invited to speak on campus to a crowd that would not embrace her on any level. She was Hanoi Jane! She was a traitor. She would not be speaking here.

During this period of time the Manson Murders were in the news, and I think Charles Manson would have been more welcome on campus than Hanoi Jane.

It seemed everywhere throughout this country there were very extreme opinions addressing common concerns. For instance, in the early 1970's Kent State was suddenly in the headlines. Student protests were conducted on campus over the bombing of Cambodia by the United States. As a result, the National Guard was ordered to Kent State by President Nixon and it was not long after that serious casualties and the loss of life on campus would be realized. Other campuses and cities nationwide had their share of protests and riots resulting in the loss of life and property.

The difficulty for me was how to discern what all of this meant to me personally. I felt I was supposed to feel like a traitor yet I felt anything but. I was confused by my lack of anger toward my government and I questioned the motives of others.

Overall I still housed very deep feelings of patriotism within.

WHAT'S UP WITH THAT?

Moving on to other matters.

Out of nowhere I would be surprised by other panic attacks. Some of them I could make sense of but for most they remained a mystery. What triggered them? Could they be attributed to campus events or world news or both? There were two reported rape cases on campus and that brought back terrible memories from my past. As much as I was trying to get beyond all this, I was failing. I must re-emphasize that this unrecognized behavior would haunt me my entire life. I am a bottom line person and have a keen talent when it comes to details. This, however, I could not figure out. What was going on with me. Feelings of concern caused me to withdraw even further. I was not only dealing with a sense of panic, but I had symptoms of being agoraphobic. And I was not just self-diagnosing. That did become a legitimate, personal diagnoses many years later.

At any rate, all of the unknowns were destroying me little by little. Being in denial about being sexually assaulted while in the military was the problem but would only be recognized as such forty-two years later.

I forced myself to mingle in public. Ultimately, I would find things to do that excluded others, which posed less of a threat to me.

My favorite place to escape to was the Anza Borrego Desert. Camping in a primitive campground was awesome. The only amenity available was an outhouse. Hurray for that "pit stop."

Camping in the high desert is quite different than camping experiences I had enjoyed over time. Blazing hot temperatures during the day and very cold temperatures at night could be expected, depending on the time of year.

When the evening weather was not so cold, I would sleep under a star-lit sky in my sleeping bag. Talk about an escape from the public, this was certainly it! There were so many stars they would literally silhouette the mountains. Even more beautiful was viewing the constant display of shooting stars. I didn't have any trouble falling asleep.

Daylight vistas proved to be entertaining in their own way. The high desert is made up of huge boulders, some tumbleweed, and various types of cacti. One day I decided to climb the boulders to catch sight of the Salton Sea. I was exhausted but the view was well worth the effort.

Other entertainment was provided by a whole cast of characters. While tending to my camp fire something caught my eye and I just stood there and gazed at the long horn sheep perched along the mountain with no fear of losing their footing. What show offs!

Not to be outdone by the long horn sheep, road runners raced onto the scene. To give you an example of how quiet it was in that area, one could hear the sound of the road runners' feet hitting the ground. Had it not been for that sound, I would have missed the show.

My most inspiring moments were lying on my cot looking up

at a rocky crag after noticing some interesting activity. For the following three or four hours I watched a mother Hawk teaching her young to fly. Their nest was right at the edge of the crag so the little birds did not have far to go to catch an updraft. One of the youngsters got caught in a pretty strong wind and began disappearing into the wild blue yonder. Momma Hawk chased after her charge and folded her wings around it and both began plummeting to the earth. Just in time, momma opened her wings to break their fall. Oh, how I ached for the freedom of the critters and the birds.

What did I learn from those magnificent moments? None of us can fly unless we first begin to fall. I reflect back to that time every so often.

I had two other places to which I would escape, both giving me a sense of calm. In the largeness of the mountains and the pacific ocean, one can find a desolate area to break away from the public. Standing before the ocean made me we want to spread my arms and embrace its glorious presentation of sky, sea and earth. The mountains, on the other hand, made me feel very small in relation to my place in the universe. It was a humbling experience and one I remind myself of at times.

Hanging on to these truths inspired by nature would not be easy. Being in denial and seeking to escape from others, would, in the long run, do me no good. I asked myself the question: "What have I done and what have I done to me?" Because I was in denial, I would be unable to answer that question until many, many years later.

LET'S GET ON WITH LIVING

At age twenty-five I knew I couldn't just sit around waiting for another panic attack. Not being able to pin-point when the attacks would visit me was beyond disturbing. Somehow I had to start living again. I had to rescue me from myself.

With mixed emotions, I re-entered the dating world. Over a three year period I dated three wonderful men and, no, not at the same time. Each of them proved to be wonderful men in regard to their characters and core values. Their social skills were of importance to me as was their senses of humor. Money has never been my motivator in life so they had to be pretty special for me to spend time with them. I wasn't a cheap date and I wasn't an out-to-break-someone's-wallet kind of date either.

You have heard: "It's not you, it's me." I had to say that more than once. I know I broke some hearts but I was not able to make a commitment to marriage. And sadly, "the one" got away as a result of my insecurities.

Dating at that point in time was a matter of having a social life without having to make a commitment. It worked for me at the time. Please do not misunderstand me, for I was not using or misleading anyone. I was dating. I made myself clear in a kind and gentle way from the beginning that I was not interested in a long-term relationship.

Surprisingly, I found the men I dated appreciated knowing my philosophy on commitment. Part of that, I believe, was a "California way of thinking." But most important: once my dates understood where I was coming from, it took some of the pressure off of them thinking they had to perform in the bedroom.

The men I dated were kind, affectionate, and generous. Further, they were always the manly man type but were not afraid to tap into the gentleness buried within them. It takes a strong man to do that. The European men seem to be way ahead of North American men in this regard.

My social life had expanded to include attending social events hosted by some of the staff, administrators, and professors at the university. My life seemed to be back on track in the social realm.

However, news from home made me extremely worried. My little sister had been divorced for a few years and dated several guys with whom she was friends from school. At some point she agreed to go out with a man quite a bit older, a local deputy sheriff. The troubling part of this relationship had multiple layers. It came to her attention that he was married and had grown children and that disturbed her deeply. She had been lied to and was hurt.

When she tried to end the relationship he became abusive and threatening towards her. Back in the day (1973) there were no stalking laws on the books, but that is exactly what he was doing. He would follow her to and from work, to parties, to the beach, and so on. For a three month period he beat her and his threats were becoming more and more hostile. He even went as far as firing some shots at her through the passenger side of her vehicle.

Be assured that both she **and my** mother filed numerous complaints and charges against him, **but to** no avail.

In talking with my sister about this horrible situation, I begged her to move to California to live with me. She responded: "I am not running from anybody." Sadly, I believe her pride cost her her life. Before ending our conversation we said : "I love you." I did not have a good feeling about her future at all.

Two weeks later, on October 7th, 1973 at 2:15am my phone rang to bring me news from my **mother** that my sister had been killed. I asked her, which one?

It was my little sister!

My brain screamed: no, no, **no, no,** NO!

The deputy sheriff (the stalker she'd tried to rid herself of) had followed her to a party, waited **for her** in the parking lot, put his weapon to her left temple, and pulled the trigger. He must have meant it when he told her: "If I **can't have** you nobody will." The police and emergency personnel **were** called to the scene and something happened that haunts **me** to this day. The ambulance attendant asked my sister's killer if **he** knew what he had done. He responded: "Yes, I killed her."

I told mom I would be on the next flight back to Florida.

I suddenly felt sick to my stomach so I went to the bathroom and leaned over the sink. I heard a loud, low sound but did not know where it was coming from.

It was me. I didn't recognize my own voice. Suddenly, I was very cold. I guess I was in shock and no matter how many blankets I piled on, I could not get warm.

The following evening I was on a plane home to bury my beautiful, fun-loving little sister. My flight home was in such contrast to what I would soon be facing on the tarmac. The skies were clean and filled with moonlight and stars. It reminded me of the high desert. I gazed out the window of the plane and wondered what kind of view my sister had of this amazing evening. I wondered if she felt our pain and sorrow. I wondered if she would come to visit me. You know what, she did. I know that sounds crazy, but in order for this phenomenon to become real one must believe in anything and everything.

DO WHAT YOU MUST DO

I was doing all I could to help with funeral arrangements but felt as though I was in a daze. Thank God we had known the funeral director all our lives and therefore placed a great deal of trust in his recommendations, and his warnings: "Do not bury her with her jewelry, grave robbers do exist."

Prior to the service, I viewed her body to make certain her hair looked nice and the dress we selected for her was complimentary. While looking at her, I would have sworn she was breathing.

Having never been through this, I just did what needed to be done.

For instance, when I called the hospital about her personal effects they said I needed to contact a different hospital. She had been treated here but her body had been taken elsewhere. One person told me to check with the emergency responders while another was telling me to contact hospital security personnel to have them check their safe for her jewelry. I was able to locate her jewelry, but nobody could tell me about the rest of her personal effects.

Realizing we were well known in town it was no surprise to see the number of mourners who attended. Over three hundred friends, family, and neighbors grieved with us. Also in attendance were her former teachers and previous employers. She was well liked and respected in the community, as were mom and dad.

I asked my mom and dad for their guidance as to what they wanted me to do if my older sister wanted to attend the service.

She did call and I asked her not to come out of respect for mom and dad. She did attend the service, but stood way off in the distance in an effort not to be seen. I felt very bad for her as she, too, was grieving. At the same time, I understood my folks in not wanting her there.

After her burial, I had to find time to grieve her death. Around dusk I returned to her grave. I just could not stand the thought of her being there all alone. I sat next to her grave and was weeping when one of her friends showed up. I was so glad she did. She was able to share some wonderfully funny stories about Angie. I think I returned home in the wee hours of the morning and expected to find mom and dad resting. Who was I kidding?

The following days were filled with very interesting events. Upon opening the mail I was looking at a $500.00 fee for medical services provided while "transporting the patient." Shame on these people! I called them and asked them about the charge and they reiterated what was on the invoice. I gave them time to hang themselves before telling them what I knew about this matter.

"Excuse me, but I have read the death certificate and the autopsy report. The 'patient' was deceased before she hit the ground and did not require any life saving efforts while being transported," I said.

Before ending my call to them I made certain they knew not to look for remittance regarding this invoice. That was the last I spoke with them.

Further dealings took my mom and me to pay off the balance owed on my sister's car. It would be given to her ex husband. Yes, they had been divorced, but remained good friends. The clerk I spoke to said that since we did not own the car she could not accept the pay-off amount on the vehicle. Huh? So, I asked to speak to the bank manager and explained what we wanted to do and that was the end of that. Mission accomplished. I feel a need to point out to you that after this incident her car had been impounded, so we had to jump through more hoops to retrieve the vehicle. We were told there was no evidence found in the vehicle and therefore they released it to our custody.

Once we got the car home, I sat inside with my hands on the steering wheel just reflecting on the person she was. Funny thing, while I was cleaning out her car I located two spent slugs in the side panels. And we were told there was no evidence found in the car? I dug them out from where they were imbedded and threw them as far as I could. Was that a mistake? Not really when you consider the rest of this terrible journey.

Now we had to attend a **preliminary** hearing to determine what my sister's killer would be **charged** with.

We and various witnesses, sat from 7:00am to 5:00pm without anyone letting us know **whether** we should stay or go. It didn't take me long to figure out what was happening. While playing the waiting game I asked where I **needed** to go to claim Angie's personal effects. Up to that point they were being held as evidence. I received some vague directions, but it became obvious I was in the wrong place. On my way back I **caught** a glimpse of my mother walking through the court yard. I could only see the very top of her head because of the height of the **hedges**, but because of her snow white hair, I knew it was her. I was **totally** puzzled and worried as to why she was out there.

When she rounded the **corner** I just wanted to wrap her in cotton to protect her from everything. She was carrying a clear plastic evidence bag containing my sister's bloody, personal effects. How mom was able to put one foot in **front** of the other is a mystery to me.

Two weeks had gone by **and** I had to return to work in

California. Being away didn't keep me from following the impending trial. Sadly, because of our financial status, a court appointed attorney was assigned to represent us.

While awaiting trial, the killer of my sister attempted suicide twice in his jail cell. Do you not think his behavior was orchestrated to influence a jury? Well, I do! He also wrote a note stating he wanted to be buried next to my sister.

Over my dead body.

We were, however, advised that if there was room in the family plot his wish would be honored. Luckily, the family plot was full.

His trial was criticized and scrutinized by many. The major complaint was about the exterior construction noise from outside the courtroom. It led some to believe the jury was unable to hear all of the proceedings.

Here is my take on this whole circus. Law enforcement was protecting one of their own and I felt that very early on in this process.

Key witnesses were not called by the prosecutor, nor were my mother, her close friends, or the ambulance driver. Not calling the ambulance driver to testify is what haunts me today and will into eternity.

We also learned during this "judicial" process that none of the complaints about the killer filed by my mother covering a three to five month period could be found. And claiming insanity seemed to be the popular thing to do to save your own butt. In the end, not one witness for the prosecution was called and, of course, the defense attorney did not call his defendant. I know all of that sounds bizarre but this will blow you out of the water. The defense attorney tried to convince the jury my sister had committed suicide. Let me ask you this very basic question: why would a right-handed individual reach around to the left temple to commit suicide by a gun shot? That's another minor detail the court appointed attorney missed.

At the end of the day, there was no <u>proof</u> that would lead him to be convicted of premeditated murder. Instead, he would be found guilty of manslaughter and sentenced to serve fifteen years in prison. Keep in mind however, it took three years to bring him to trial and that counted toward time served. Did law enforcement protect one of their own? I believe so. Did his sentence make a difference to our family? Absolutely it did. Blame it on whatever. Dead is dead.

During this time, I lost all respect for the judicial system and I have never been able to reclaim the concept of justice for all.

This horrible event destroyed my family. We were all grieving so we found it impossible to turn to each other for comfort. We were all angry yet didn't know where to direct that very strong emotion, and we were all running on empty.

During the period my sister was being threatened and abused my mother did not share it with my father for fear of what he might do. As a result, dad blamed mom for my sister's death and it couldn't get any worse than that. Because of the polarization between my parents they would ultimately divorce. Thirty-three years shared and thirty-three years lost. That's extremely sad I think.

How in the world was I to get on with living? I too was running on empty.

LIFE DOES GO ON

Believe it or not, like it or not, life does go on. And I am here to tell you it is not easy finding a way to put one foot in front of the other.

I can also tell you there is no manual guiding you through the grieving process. And, there is no right way or wrong way to grieve. Because we are all different, we cannot be expected to grieve as though we have been cloned. There is no timeline carved in stone as to when you must begin grieving or when you should have moved beyond the grief or the terrible void you are coping with on a daily basis.

Returning to my job at the university left me little time to grieve and in a way I was thankful for that. However, well-meaning friends and associates pressed me for details of my sister's death. They were not trying to be rude, it just came out that way. At any rate, I couldn't escape the realness of those awkward moments. I had to find a way to grieve and I had to do it my way.

I believe I was in a state of shock for a period of time and in hind-sight I viewed that as a blessing. And I was ready to accept all of the blessings I could get. Large, medium or small, it didn't matter to me. Just send them my way.

This was not my first exposure to losing someone to sudden death, but that doesn't make it any easier. I must have been around the age of ten when my maternal grandmother suddenly died of a cerebral hemorrhage. At that age I knew she had died and I watched family members weep but I didn't really grasp the seriousness of it all. I just knew I missed her dearly.

Adapt and overcome is the answer to many difficult situations if you want to believe the Marine Corps philosophy. Yes, it was the way for me to begin grieving. I had to look at all of the "it could be worse" stuff to get me on the road to being whole again.

Having served during the Vietnam Conflict I had plenty to reflect upon. All I had to do was begin the process. So let's begin.

Michelle F. Capucci

HIDDEN DANGERS

While working for the Chief of Staff, one of my responsibilities was to update daily a huge volume of information pertaining to various aspects on matters relating to Vietnam. All I had to do was remove the old informational page and replace it with the most current information. Within some of these pages were photographs of the jungles identifying numerous booby-traps. Looking at those photos challenged me to identify as many of those booby-traps as I could. I failed miserably. Tunnels used by the Viet Cong to move about unseen were not seen by my eye and neither were the c-ration cans used to injure whomever it was that would step on a trip wire. Not being trained in this particular phase of my enlistment, I did not feel too badly about not seeing what was really right in front of me. Once I began working with the photos and asking the men I worked with about them, it improved my skills in identifying booby-traps.

We, this country, had never fought this kind of enemy in this particular venue. We had a great deal to learn if our men were to come home alive. Camp Pendleton created a Vietnam Village to simulate what our men would be facing once deployed. It proved to be quite helpful.

After having said all that, let me share another responsibility I was tasked with at the same time. Everyday brought more news of deaths. My task was to ensure that the families of these fallen men received a letter of condolence from "a grateful nation." I further processed the autopsy reports to ensure they were complete and accurate with regard to name, rank, and service number, etc. I didn't have to read them but I felt an obligation to do so out of respect.

The autopsy reports were very graphic. If our fallen hero had stepped on a land mine the autopsy report gave a detailed picture of what had happened. Torso located 22 degrees northwest, left ankle located 17 degrees east, right arm located 9 degrees south, but unable to locate right foot.

Yes, these men were put in body bags for further processing. Burial details nationwide were kept very busy with making certain these men of honor were laid to rest with the greatest of respect.

My office window overlooked Arlington National Cemetery and the visual of a military funeral is quite impressive, as it should be.

During this period of time Arlington Cemetery, on average, was conducting thirty funerals a day. Let me take you there. It is winter, the trees are bare of their leaves, and there is snow on the ground. There is no hiding the fact that there is a flag-draped caisson moving through the cemetery. That flag took center stage on this particular day in that it was my first experience in observing this kind of burial. The Red, White and Blue were the only colors noticeable in that setting. I had to catch my breath when I noticed the riderless horse with the boots facing backwards. When *Taps* was played it could be heard by all as was the three-volley salute preceding the playing of *Taps*. With the trees having dropped their leaves there was nothing to mute the sound of *Taps*. I said a silent prayer for the family of this person who lost his life fighting to preserve our freedom.

What does this have to do with the death of my sister? Everything if you consider what was best for me in beginning the grieving process. I had to put things in perspective, I had to balance grief in my own mind and heart and I could not do that without considering what others had suffered.

Looking back at the number of friends, relatives, and acquaintances, 300 plus, who came to pay their respects to my family, can you imagine the endless number of people wrapped in grief throughout this terrible "conflict?"

I was thankful my sister's body was in one piece and while she was transitioning from this life to the next I know she felt loved. Reflecting back allowed me to begin the grieving process. I don't guarantee this will work for anybody but me. I just wanted to share this experience with you in the hope it may lead you to a starting point.

A year or two passed and I was still being irritated and aggravated by whatever it was that would not seem to let me go. I can tell you this: more and more I was resentful of authority. No, this is

not a good thing when one is working for those in authority.

LIFE DOES GO ON, CONTINUED

Working in the university environment always proved to be interesting from day to day. Some of the Resident Assistants kept me on my toes with their off-the-wall stories or various antics.

For the holidays our office, Dean of Student Affairs, would hold an open house for the students just to give them a sense of something other than studying. Some of the students would even volunteer to help with preparing refreshment. Yep, the punch was spiked and the brownies contained wacky weed. No wonder they were so popular.

Other students would pull up a chair to my desk just to chat. I always felt complimented by that because I felt it meant they trusted me enough to share their concerns.

One student, a senior at the time, was so looking forward to having her grandmother at her graduation ceremony. There was only one problem, but it was a big one. His name was Fidel Castro. This student, a young lady of Cuban descent, did everything possible to bring her grandmother to the United States. She wanted her eighty six year old grandmother to know freedom. However, the Cuban government felt she might pose a threat to the Castro Regime. No, she was not successful in getting her grandmother out of Cuba.

Another young lady became pregnant and was on the verge of doing something she may have regretted. Keep in mind the University of San Diego is a Catholic University, and we know what the ism on abortion was at this point in time. She and I would talk on numerous occasions as she wrestled with making a decision that would certainly impact her future.

My personal view: there is always the option of placing an infant up for adoption in lieu of being pressured into having an abortion. Back in the day, many of those decisions were made out of fear of what one's family and friends would think about a pregnancy out of wedlock. Even if the couple were to marry, people would start counting on their fingers to see if all of the facts fit when pinning down the due date.

My involvement consisted of providing this young, bright student with information that would give her options. I gave her phone numbers to call and pointed her in the direction of people with whom she could discuss this very sensitive matter. Obviously, she could not go to the nuns.

The information I gave her provided her with names and places of legitimate agencies dedicated not only to helping her emotionally, but financially. She was given the option of having her baby, but would have to travel to Northern California. This was strictly for the purpose of protecting her privacy. The young woman did have her child, knowing the adoptive parents had agreed to pay her medical expenses. Within an acceptable amount of time she returned to resume her education. Yes, I believe she made a very wise decision, and so did she.

At this point I am five years into my tenure with the university and some interesting things are happening. Those things certainly didn't make me happy, nor others in an administrative support role.

Whenever a vacancy occurred through attrition, the newly hired personnel were brought in at a higher level of pay than those with tenure. I jokingly said to my boss: "It seems the thing for me to do is resign and then reapply to enjoy a pay raise."

The following day I began thinking about what I had said and realized he did not respond to my comment. I was not at all happy with what I perceived to be happening. After having talked with other support staff, I learned I was not alone in feeling "used and abused" by our respective bosses.

This situation became the final straw for me. I walked out of the office at 10:00am. and did not return. I quit!

Now I had no job, no car, and no desire to ever be in an unemployment line again.

Not long after, I received a phone call from a former classmate letting me know about a job opportunity with the Navy Resale System back on the East Coast. I was given a telephone interview and was offered the job demanding a two-week start up time.

Within a week, I was relocating to the East Coast to begin working in the Personnel Department for the Navy Resale System at NOB in Norfolk, Virginia.

CULTURE SHOCK

The average temperature in San Diego is seventy-six degrees. The Pacific Ocean is breathtakingly beautiful with its various shades of blue. Sunsets are captivating and the mountains truly majestic. There is little humidity, even during Santa Ana conditions, meaning even at 114 degrees one does not feel like the heat will kill them at any given moment. On a day absent the smog blowing in from Los Angeles, you can see the Mexican peninsula and points beyond. There is no need to spend money on a charter boat to enjoy whale watching. It is possible to just stand on the shore and enjoy the event during the migration season. Most night skies are filled with a magnificent display of the heavens. The moonlight will invariably highlight the breaking surf, which seems to marry with the shore as it washes in with lace-like foam.

The East Coast however, is a different story. When I boarded the plane headed east the temperature was seventy-four degrees. When I landed at Norfolk International Airport the temperature was five degrees! Trust me when I tell you nothing about my wardrobe prepared me for this moment.

The trip from the airport was uneventful except for my reaction to seeing so many trees. They were everywhere. There were so many, they blocked the view of the horizon. I know that sounds strange, but it was such a contrast to the West Coast. My eyes were longing for the horizon.

My high school friend, who had made me aware of the job at NOB, came with her husband to meet me at the airport. We immediately headed for my new living arrangement, their home, and what a home it was.

My friends were in transition, too. They were building a new house on four acres of land in the country. No, I was not made aware of this until we pulled into their temporary habitat: an overgrown driveway that ran parallel to an old farm house. The old farmhouse was just that: old. And next to the farmhouse were my new digs

Three adults, a standard size poodle, and an Afghan hound would all be staying together in a twelve by twenty-two foot trailer until the new house was finished. Don't forget: the temperature is five degrees. Do you have any idea how uncomfortable that can be in a trailer?

Inside this mini-mansion were two cots and a futon, which would serve as my bed. And it was the bed the Afghan opted to share with me. Luckily, she provided much-needed body heat. The trailer also had a tiny bathroom, a tiny table, and a tiny stove. I felt like I was in munchkin land.

The cook stove was gas operated. At first, we dared not try lighting it, for fear there may have been an airlock in the line due to the temperature. But we needed to defrost our toothpaste, so we took the risk. The dogs' dishes had frozen to the floor. Snow was in the forecast. Oh goodie!

Later, the pipes froze which gave us a tiny flood in the tiny bathroom. We needed a way to redirect the water. Being the geniuses we were, we duck-taped a douche-bag to the broken area of the pipe, then directed the bag's wand back into the sink. In essence, we just kept recycling the water.

In case you are unaware, a trailer has a holding tank to contain human waste, and it requires emptying every so often. Two of us would have to carry a full bucket to a septic area where we'd slip and slop on the frozen ground, inventing a few expletives in the process.

My camping buddies and I ate, slept, shared a ride to work, and defrosted pipes for a period of six months while waiting for the house to be completed. Surprisingly, we did not get on each other's nerves, and before we knew it, it was moving day.

As with most moves one enlists all the free labor possible. Good friends, family members, work associates, and comrades in arms. I forgot to mention my friends' husband was serving in the Navy. At any rate, I believe we have all heard the old adage: "nothing is free." You guessed it – our free labor cost us our pride and reputations as good neighbors when they accidentally set the property aflame.

To explain: as we unpacked our respective boxes we would toss them out of the back sliding glass doors with the request that some of the crew break them down for disposal. But instead of following our directions, some of the free labor decided it was more efficient to burn the boxes. There were a couple of things that went wrong with that approach. One should never start a ground fire without some sort of protective barrier, and one should never ever start a ground fire on a windy day.

Okay, so now the property is on fire, we have no phone service to call for help, and our nearest neighbors are four acres away. I raced next door traveling down a five foot deep ditch and up the other side with the hope somebody would be home to alert the fire department. Luckily, there was, and she happened to be the wife of an active firefighter. Needless to say, her call was expedited through the normal channels for immediate dispatch.

Here's the thing. County living does not always have some of the important perks made available to city folk. Like what? Like a fire hydrant!

To contain this blaze a self-contained ATV was dispatched which seemed to get the job done. Our new neighbor just looked at us in disbelief and warmly identified us as "city slickers." That evening, my two housemates decided to go the local bar & grill while I stayed home to relish the solitude.

My living space was their garage, converted for my comfort. I had three tall book cases I configured to use as a room divider separating my living space from my sleeping space. On either side of the sofa I had two table lamps that had a smoke-gray design with flickering bulbs engaged with a three-way switch. With my feet kicked up and listening to some music, I kept seeing a flickering light that I thought was the table lamps. Not so! Upon further inspection I realized the fire from earlier had not been extinguished.

Still having no phone service, I once again had to charge across four acres of land, down and up the same deep ditch (this time it was very, very dark outside) for the purpose of having the fire department make a return trip. Did I forget to mention there were reports of Big Foot?!

The following morning we were all sitting at the breakfast bar when we noticed more smoke from outside. With a five-gallon bucket and shovel in hand we headed out to finally put this fire out. I don't know how deep we had to dig to achieve our goal of extinguishing the smoldering underground fire, but we did it. And, yes, we still carry the name "city slickers."

Moving back east was like traveling back in time some seventeen years or more. The culture shock I had been exposed to at this point became more intense when I was forced to face matters that had not been a part of my life for a very long time.

I had been less aware of racial prejudices while living out west, and I now found its presence very disturbing. Keep in mind I already had ongoing issues with trust, fear, loud noises, and being around strangers.

At this point in time a movie called *Roots* was playing. It seemed to make matters worse in regard to the racial divide and prejudicial attitudes in general. As I said previously, I was not used to this kind of demeanor between two separate races or cultures nor did

I embrace the attitudes being displayed.

As the seasons changed I was aware of an even more quirky east coast reality. Can somebody explain to me why in the heat and humidity of summer men wear three-piece suits?

Can somebody tell my why people on the West Coast say: "turn off the lights" but people on the East Coast say: "cut off the lights?" I always expected to see somebody racing toward the light switch with a machete. Even more puzzling to me: folks out West say: "I'd be happy to take you to the store" but the East Coast folks say: "I'd be happy to run you to the store."

I guess it is true. East is East and West is West and never the twain shall meet.

While living in the country, we worked very hard to establish a yard (not a lawn) that was somewhat green. We also built a pole barn for the horses and added a dog run that the goat could enjoy. It just seemed to me that the culture shock was so much more than my new living environment verses my working environment at the base. I am not complaining. I am merely attempting to show the contrast of my two different worlds at this point in time.

One afternoon, on my way home from work, I stopped by the Municipal Center and submitted an application for employment with the Personnel Department. My resume' was printed on bright yellow paper so as to not be overlooked, or so I thought. A week or so went by before I called to inquire about the status of my application. Not long after I was scheduled for an interview at 4:00pm the following day. The interview continued into the 6:00pm hour, but was concluded when I asked directions to the ladies room. At round 7:30pm I received a call offering me the job. I accepted. Here's the strange part of all of this: the interview was dominated with talk about the basketball team from my interviewer's college. Bar none, it was the most absurd interview I had experienced.

This particular job, although I took a cut in pay to accept the position, was much closer to home. I was looking forward to not having to get up at 4:00am to be at work by 7:00am.

IS THIS FOR REAL?

I should have known from my initial interview that this was going to be a job from hell. Instead, it took me a week to realize the Department of Personnel was a finger pointing environment. This puzzled me because, in my opinion, if one is doing one's job there is nothing to hide or run from. Apparently, my new colleagues had not learned that.

Early on in the hiring process, it had been revealed to me that my resume had been sent to the circular file because of my military experience. Could it be that a draft dodger placed it there? I didn't know, but the gesture offended me.

The staff member I replaced had apparently alienated

everyone she worked with. I know it took a good six months for me to win the staff's respect and trust. Before that, my calls to staff were met with: "What did I do wrong?"

My job involved daily interaction with many departments within the organization. Yet I found little direction or guidance. There was no training offered, so I made a point to pay close attention to detail. Still, it often felt like I was flying blind. I processed detailed data on all personnel records, evaluations, unemployment hearings, and much more. It all came close to killing me. During the course of working there, two doctors recommended I leave due to stress-related issues. I would later take their advice, but not before living with elevated blood pressure for years.

It was around this time that I met and fell in love with a wonderful man--or so I thought. We soon began all the necessary requirements to be married in the Catholic Church. We had it all: church, priests, guests, and reception, with plans for a four day honeymoon in picturesque Colonial Williamsburg.

We were back in two.

The brevity of our honeymoon caused me to question his

commitment to our "union." It did not take long for me to realize I had married Jekyll and Hyde.

On the afternoon we arrived home he sat on the sofa with his legs and arms crossed and announced: "I should tell you I have serious doubts about being married again."

I don't know if that confession was meant to pave the way for him to be unfaithful, which he was, but my mind kept hearing him say the word "again."

Within the next three months, I discovered some interesting things my new husband had neglected to share. It seems he had been married before and had had a daughter. I can't tell you how it felt to realize I was his second wife.

Time went on and things went from bad to worse. He was unfaithful. Honestly, I don't know how some women can find the strength to forgive their spouses when they know they have cheated. They are stronger than I am.

After a year of separation, our divorce became final. On that very day he was already taking his third wife, and I was on a plane to San Diego to be with good, solid friends. I had also begun annulment proceedings.

The following year my annulment was approved by Rome, with the suggestion that I should consider marrying again, and also seek counseling.

Say What?

I guess they didn't know it was my loving husband who needed counseling.

Everything happens for a reason and I was about to make some sense out of it all.

After my mom and dad divorced both were able to find gentleness and affection in others. My mother's companion died suddenly of a heart attack and that left her living alone, something she had never done. I phoned her and invited her to come live with me. I explained that my marriage had failed and that I wanted to give her a safe place to live. She was hesitant to accept, thinking I could salvage my marriage. She didn't want to interfere. Having convinced her my time spent in "wedded bliss" was over, I made plans to fly to Florida to help her pack and get her on a new path.

Let me remind you that mom had always been stay-at-home.

So it was going to be interesting trying to find work for her. She was fifty-two years old when she came to live with me, and she wanted to work and pay her own way.

Her biggest obstacle was in feeling she had no marketable skills. She pictured herself doing menial tasks. That didn't bother her, but I knew she had more to offer. Being the good personnel employee I was, I sat with her one evening and went over all the skills she possessed simply by being a stay-at-home mom. Multitasking was her biggest asset, but was not the most important. Moms do all kinds of things we do in the workforce but they are not paid. It was now time for my mom to get paid for her knowledge, skills, and abilities.

When she applied for work in local government, I went to those who would be administering tests and interviewing her. I emphasized she should be treated like any other applicant. She landed the job and I could not have been more proud.

She was hired as a part-time receptionist, but within a short period of time garnered a full-time position. Go mom! She worked in a very large department and, of course, had to become "mom" to all of them.

Twelve years later she would die of lung cancer. Out of deep respect and affection, her co-workers pitched in to have a bald cypress planted in her honor. If you are familiar with that tree you understand it will stand for a very long time.

I want to stop at this point to share a story with you that I hope will reveal to you the beauty of my mother.

On several occasions, the department in which mom worked offered her a better position and higher pay. She came home one evening and seemed troubled so we ate dinner and talked about her concerns. Bless her heart, she didn't want a better position or higher pay. But she didn't want to disappoint me or her co-workers. It didn't take long for me to convince her that she was where she was meant to be and that she shouldn't feel pressured by anybody or anything.

In the short period of time my mother lived with me, I observed a miracle. I watched her find her way out of her cocoon to become a beautiful butterfly. As a matter of fact, I gave her a butterfly net for her birthday one year and she smiled with such love in her eyes.

My employment in "personnel" lasted eighteen miserable years before I finally took the doctors' advice and left. I'd been struggling over what to do for a long time.

I came home one evening from a difficult day at work, sat outside, and gathered my thoughts. I considered the possibilities for my future. Should I stay or should I go? I was conflicted. At that moment, a monarch butterfly appeared, and I could hear my mother saying: "it's not worth it."

With that, I retired at age forty-nine from this terrible job and began working for myself in the housekeeping business.

When I left, it was easy to withdraw from the people I worked with. My symptoms of panic and anxiety were always with me. The immense building with its endless hallways and claustrophobic elevators. The nebulous staff meetings. I'd always felt trapped. Did I confide to anyone about these moments of fear and anxiety? How could I? I was not able to name my problem for many years.

Please understand I am not bearing my soul to solicit pity or sympathy from you. That is the last thing I want. My hope is that as you read you can find within yourself an inner strength you have yet to tap. I hope to inspire you to dig deep inside to discover the person you are meant to be.

My journey, however, is not over. I am traveling a road that is frightening because I don't know what it is I am facing. I am striving to put a name on it, and I am having to deal with it again and again.

I will learn it's name is MST (Military Sexual Trauma), and I can assure you it has had a profound impact on my life.

LET'S LOOK BACK

I enlisted in the United States Marine Corps in 1966. I raised my hand and swore to "support and defend the Constitution of the United States against all enemies, foreign and domestic." What a proud moment that was and is for all who have taken the oath regardless of the branch of service we joined. Taking that oath brings us to the immediate realization that, if necessary, we are expected to die for our country.

1966 gave us continued involvement in the Vietnam Conflict. Attitudes were anything but supportive of those of us in uniform. We did, however, serve with pride. We believed we were doing the right thing by serving our country, yet we were met with contradictory behavior from many fellow Americans. To say the least, it was difficult and challenging to sort through all the chaos within our own country. Chaos pitting us against our friends and neighbors due to opposing views. Being spat upon, having to field thrown bottles, food, and being called a "baby killer" was not something I was prepared for. I witnessed marches on the Pentagon, burning and looting of businesses in D.C., bathing in the Reflection Pool, numerous protests, and much, much more.

Serving with pride and doing the uniform justice became my goal. Against enormous odds I focused on my own deep feelings of patriotism to guide me.

But let's focus on the language: "against all enemies, foreign and domestic." There is no other way to say this: I was not expecting an enemy from within — but it came. It came in the form of Military Sexual Assault.

I am not talking about sexual harassment. I am talking about sexual assault. Put simply: if someone touches you without your consent, you are being assaulted. And I will argue that point with anyone. So I met the "enemy from within." Now what do I do about it?

Trust me when I tell you this: you must meet the matter head on. Otherwise, your feelings will only get worse. The trauma suffered will manifest itself in one way or another. You may become hyper-vigilant, exhausted from constantly scrutinizing your surroundings. For me, the most damaging manifestation appeared as distrust. Forming or maintaining important or meaningful relationships seemed impossible. I didn't want to believe what had happened. That, my friends, we call denial.

I filed a formal complaint, yet my words fell on deaf ears. I asked the investigators: "Did you hear me?"

Word got around. I became withdrawn. I became antisocial. I hid from the continual insults, cat calls, unpleasant sexual overtones, and unfounded accusations.

Becoming antisocial felt safe, but was also pretty lonely. Yet it gave me time to process what I was experiencing.

Allegedly, I was the problem. Oh yes I was! You see, women almost always ask to be assaulted, or so a great many folks told me. And yep – they were mostly men.

WHAT DID YOU SAY OR DO?

If you go through this demeaning experience you will be asked: "Did you say no?"

Give me a break!

Don't think that just because you report this to the proper authorities things will get better. They will not! They will ask you: Did you say no? Did you say stop? Did you tell anyone? Do you have a witness? Did you go to work? Did you get a physical? And on and on it goes.

The tone of these questions is insulting and accusatory. And I don't care how you respond to these inquiries--you will not be believed. Your responses will be twisted, challenged, and given little

186

to no credence or value.

Did you Hear Me?

Back in the day, there were no military guidelines for handling this very sensitive matter. Because I took the proactive step of reporting my experience, my career was immediately jeopardized. My Top Secret clearance was also jeopardized, which, of course, was unacceptable.

A long story short: it was not fashionable to seek help, i.e. counseling, in the 1960s. Instead, counseling carried a huge stigma and implied one was not fit to serve. But if someone didn't seek help, then there must have been no suffering, pain, or duress. A true catch 22. Suffice it to say, it was a very different time in our social history, and in how sexual assault was managed — or not.

Michelle F. Capucci

NO MYSTERY

Can somebody tell me how the basic right/wrong tenets of our values were overlooked/dismissed? I can. It was intentional.

WHO HAD I BECOME?

It was now clear to me that Military Sexual Assault was and is an extremely well kept secret and that is not by accident.

No, I am not a trained psychologist, psychiatrist, or social worker. But I would be willing to bet that people abusing people in the military probably exhibit that same behavior as civilians.

Manifestations in coping with this trauma may include self-medicating with drugs or alcohol, or even severe depression from playing the self-blame game. You may find yourself asking: "What did I do or say that allowed this to happen?"

Knowing now what I did not know then, I ask myself: "How did becoming antisocial provide a feeling of safety?" and "Why was being social so threatening to me?"

Long story short: a port in the storm was not to be found.

I experienced these side-effects as a result of being sexually assaulted. The symptoms were subtle and appeared without warning. I would blame a not-so-good day on a restless night, or my work load, or not enough coffee, blah, blah, blah. I simply did not know what I was dealing with. I had this issue so buried and disguised to protect myself from pain that I became my own worst enemy.

I learned to distrust everyone, and most of all myself. I suddenly found I had little to no respect for authority. I began drinking. Drinking, I believed, would allow me to sleep without having nightmares. Sometimes, yes. Sometimes, no. In other words: alcohol was not the answer. But what was?

In order for you to understand what I am about to share with you, we have to fast forward about 35 years.

CONFLICTING EMOTIONS

I believe everything happens for a reason and in it's own time. But I often wonder what my life might have been like had I not stuffed these feelings away. What could I have achieved if only I'd been able to trust and believe in the safety of my environment. Obviously, I will never know. And while I don't dwell incessantly on the thought of what if? I do have resentments that I must give attention to. Do I feel slighted or cheated by what this terrible act forced me to accept as part of my daily life? Absolutely. You must understand that emotional conflict becomes a dominant player under these circumstances.

Michelle F. Capucci

WHAT IS REALITY?

Having sought professional help as recently as a few years ago, I again believed I was not being heard. Sharing sensitive emotions were met with silence. Asking "did you hear me?" was also met with silence. More important, I began wondering and questioning a great many things. For instance: what is reality?

Is it what you are introduced to by the professionals, theories, studies, and lab tests? Or is it what dwells inside of you. For me, the answer was inside, but was too well hidden. For a long time it became impossible for me to identify what was real. That personal struggle led me in many directions and to this day cannot be explained easily.

Questioning my faith was the most difficult thing to balance. Did I blame God? Maybe for a period of time. But I came to understand that blaming Him was just an easy way to cope. The reality for me is that mankind was created with a free will. My attacker exercised free will. It is as simple and as real at that!

Coming to understand this truth was extremely important. There was no more blaming God.

So now what?

Well, once again, I had to walk an unknown path to discover what I was seeking: reality. Whatever that is.

I was just beginning to learn that it takes a great deal of courage to face reality.

IT IS CALLED TRAUMA

Yes, I tried counseling, group therapy, hypnosis, and meditation without feeling I had made any progress in identifying what I was dealing with.

While antidepressants were recommended, I refused to accept that directive. Masking the symptoms was not my goal. I needed to understand what I'd been dealing with all these years.

It is called trauma!

I had hidden and suppressed this for many, many years and now it was time to deal with it. This created even more trauma. In essence, a clinical setting, for lack of a better term, was not for me. At times I believed I was a source of entertainment for these professionals. Group therapy, in my opinion, presented an entire cast of various characters. So already entertainment was being provided.

A rant: Professional counselors throw a bunch of people who don't know or trust each other into the same room so that they can spill their guts. I don't know how they think this is helpful.

For some folks this may be the answer to some specific need that I am not aware of because I am not them. I cannot see the benefit in having someone hash and rehash painful events that bring them to a near breakdown or fits of anger over long periods of time if there is not some degree of healing. What is the point? Is it entertainment? Is it providing job security for someone? Is it a sincere effort to bring comfort, insight, understanding, and truth to this horrible offense against women serving in the armed services of the United States of America? Judging by how well kept and hidden this subject is, I would venture to say no. Once more, it seems to provide entertainment to those posing as the we-give-a-damn people. Without question this cast of characters recognizes trauma. They are the traumatized. They should not be expected to be entertaining.

YOU GOT MY BACK

What put me on the path to discovering the person of me?

Approximately ten years ago I was meeting with some fellow-veterans. The conversation was pretty much centered on their experiences in dealing with war, a myriad of injuries, PTSD, and so on. One of the Vets shared a story about an injury he sustained from falling off the back of a truck while serving in Iraq. He asked if I had ever been injured while serving on active duty. I hesitated to answer because I thought he was talking about combat injuries. As it turns out, his question was not limited to suffering a combat injury.

My answer was yes. I explained I had gone head over heels down a flight of stairs while at work. He then encouraged me to file a claim with the VA for compensation as a result of that injury and the long-term effects I have endured as a result of that fall.

He then asked me a question that took me aback. Were you ever abused or sexually assaulted while serving on active duty? Oh my God. Was this obvious? After spending so much energy hiding this ugly event, how did he know to ask me that question? Now my head was spinning. After a long pause my answer again was yes. Suddenly I felt exposed, threatened, insecure, angry, hurt — you name it. I was smothered in every emotion known.

Following his advice, I filed a claim for both injuries.

The following year brought some interesting news. My claim from falling down the stairs was approved for compensation. But my claim for PTSD as a result of Military Sexual Trauma (MST) was disapproved.

That decision left me believing I had just been called a liar!

As a result, I filed an appeal. It was a journey I did not want to begin. I did not believe I had the strength to put one foot in front of the other. But neither did I want to be called a liar. Thus, my difficult trek began. I compare this to a forced march. It is just something one must do.

It is here the navigator enters the picture. DAV (Disabled American Veterans) is a wonderful organization. They work tirelessly to meet the needs of many veterans. So is AMVETS. I tapped the resource of both organizations but opted to use AMVETS for a singular reason: I would be communicating with a woman and not a man. Certainly you understand the why of my decision. Come on? Was I expected to share intimate details of sexual assault with a male? Do I need to expound? I didn't think so.

My introduction to this process was interesting to say the least.

The National Center for PTSD, as well as the VA, recognizes Military Sexual Trauma as a real issue. How can that be if the brass spends so much energy hiding this offense?

As an aside, I object to the term disorder. Post Traumatic Stress is an injury requiring treatment. It is not a disorder. It seemed I was awakening to a world I had never known. I began to wonder if anyone had my back.

GET NAVIGATIONAL HELP

Deciding to tap the resource of a navigator is a decision you will not regret. By the way, I use the term navigator because that is exactly what veterans organizations do. They navigate the unfamiliar waters for you.

With your approval, you allow them to act on your behalf by granting them Power of Attorney. Once you do that it feels as though somebody threw you a life raft.

Okay, so now you have a navigator and a life raft all in one person. Oh, I know there are probably a few others working on your behalf, but, more likely than not you will want to deal solely with your navigator. But do not think for one moment your role is to sit back and wait for them to do all the work. No way! If your representative is earning her paycheck, she should already have you working on gathering needed information. And just when you believe there is no further information to furnish: surprise! You will be asked for more.

In essence, your navigator is equal to an attorney without fees. How nice is that? I'll tell you: you will not be faced with having to say "I can no longer afford your services." All you must do is continue the march and place your trust in your navigator. They know far more than we do when it comes to these matters.

PAIN/ANXIETY/DESPAIR

Here's where the real work, pain, anxiety, and despair begins. I don't want to make this sound like a twelve-step program, but you must take one day at a time and then let it go until tomorrow. Yes, this can be a long arduous journey and I guarantee it will not be fun. If your navigator gives you homework to do, then do it! Believe it or not, you will be able to control the pace of this process to a large degree. Do not give up. It will be very tempting, but do not give up!

So now I had submitted everything in writing, or so I thought, to my navigator. But when we next spoke she said: "I want you to dig real deep and tell me what you find." I thought she was crazy and I was already emotionally spent. As it turns out, she remembered a telephone conversation we'd once had. Because she was listening, she recalled information I had revealed to her that I had overlooked, forgotten, or dismissed. Did she hear me? Yes. And thank God she did because it became the turning point in my claim.

An aside: Years later, my navigator shared with me that at first she believed my claim to be weak and was not enthusiastic about its approval. Needless to say, I was appreciative of her honesty. I was thankful she waited to tell me about her doubts. If she had told me her feelings at the time I may have quit, even though I knew I shouldn't. And no, she did not give up either. But because I had buried these matters so deep, I was not capable of revealing the necessary information at the same pace that she was working. So I began digging deeper.

Surprise!

I found all sorts of things that seemed to serve as an awakening. Photographs, newspaper clippings, names, dates, locations, special events, and yes — a witness. All of it led me to unearth what I had buried. What a painful discovery!

Looking deeper without fear, I believe I experienced an

epiphany. Suddenly, I knew what I had been dealing with for such a long time. It is called trauma. I felt as if I was drowning in an angry sea of emotions. I felt as if I had been whisked back in time 42 years by some time warp. Most of what I was having to face I did not want to understand or accept.

Once again, I found myself seeking a safe place.

THE FORCED MARCH

No, that is not the end of the journey. Matter of fact, the most difficult part of the journey was just beginning. How can that be?

In the here and now, it was time for me to deal with the cause and side effects of the trauma I had been suffering. And, I had to prove to the powers that be that I was not, am not, a liar. I knew I was preparing to dress in full gear and begin a forced march. Where would the strength and stamina come from? How was I to focus on what I knew would be a very trying and difficult trek? My brain had shut out, in a protective fashion, most of what I was not able to process for many years. But now, facing what was fearful was unavoidable and there was no escaping the ugliness of it all.

NOT AGAIN

Needless to say, I was advised to return to counseling. Oh, how I hated that! I was again expected to share all sorts of thoughts and feelings with people I didn't know or trust. Although I knew my navigator was working in my best interests, I was skeptical of her expectations. As I said previously, I didn't trust anyone anymore.

Nightmare after nightmare after nightmare haunted me as a result of revisiting this horrible event. In my dreams, my attacker had no face, was always dressed in black, and seemed to enjoy being menacing. Each nightmare provided no escape from harm, only a feeling of panic. Just as my attacker had no face, I had no voice. As much as I wanted to scream my way out of those nightmares, I had no voice! Why? Because my attacker came from behind and knocked the wind from my lungs. I had no voice!

At one point, I had to discontinue therapy. The process, the counseling, the atmosphere, the frequency was destroying me.

I made a sad discovery: some folks enjoy being a victim. Not me. I could not continue revisiting this weekly or monthly or at all. So I did the courteous thing and advised my counselor in writing that I was leaving therapy.

A few years later I was again encouraged to return to therapy as part of the process in evaluating my claim. And of course, since I did not want to be thought of as a liar, I returned to therapy. If you've never been in therapy, just imagine yourself being under a microscope. They gaze and dissect you at every turn. It is not welcoming. It is intrusive and demeaning.

YES, AGAIN

Here we go: "Tell me about your childhood, your mom and dad, your siblings, etcetera." Honestly, I don't know how many times I had to state to these professionals that I had a great childhood. Mom and Dad were always supportive of my goals and aspirations. As for my siblings: we actually liked each other. My family ate meals together and enjoyed the holidays together. We laughed and cried together at the appropriate times and we were well-known and respected within our community.

Was anybody listening to what I was saying? Are you kidding? It seems to me our families get blamed for a lot of things they are not responsible for. Is it easier to start with the family theory than to listen? Apparently so.

Having set the record straight that my family was not to blame for my situation, that meant another probable cause had to be explored.

Counselor: Did you say No?

Victim: No

Counselor: Why not?

Victim: Because I couldn't.

Counselor: What do you mean?

Victim: I was attacked from behind, thrown against a wall and had the breath knocked out of me. I could not speak at all! I was then carried into the bedroom and thrown on a bed, still unable to breathe properly.

Counselor: What did you do?

Keep in mind I am talking to a male counselor at this point. Reluctantly, I shared the gory details. But I was extremely angry with the entire setting and at what seemed to be entertaining for my counselor.

Victim: ...and then, after disposing of my bloody clothes, I took a shower and went to work.

Suck it up, Marine!

Did the guys I worked with know about this? You betcha! My attacker was proud of his "tale' and they chose to believe his story. According to him, everything was consensual. With that lie, my fellow marines expressed their disappointment in me with all kinds of unchecked comments. I had to tolerate their insults and innuendos because they didn't know the real facts.

If you have ever needed the services of a VA hospital or clinic you know that one seldom, if ever, sees the same doctor. This is true no matter the issue or treatment. In these circumstances, understanding this fact before seeking treatment is crucial to your sanity. You will face the "can I trust you" trip over and over again.

And so I did. But I had a big frown across the breadth of my heart. Overall, I am not a negative person. When I can, I dismiss myself from all energy that is not positive. Yes, I can find the answer to why I am that way without help. It is just who I am. How beautifully simple is that?

Next question.

Counselor: Did you report this to anyone?

Victim: Yes

Counselor: To whom did you report this?

Victim: My roommate, my priest, and my bosses.

Notice the word boss is plural. And as I've already stated, I filed a formal complaint with Navy Central Intelligence Service (NCIS).

Between you, the reader, and me, the only person listening to what I had to say was my roommate. Or if others were listening, I was not aware of their concern.

Oh, let me rephrase that. My bosses and my priest listened but could only point out that if I pursued the matter further it would jeopardize my career. They did not, however, offer any recommendations about a solution to the matter. That, of course, is not surprising. Also, as previously stated, there were no guidelines to follow. No "recommended criteria" offering a resolution, nor the answer to the question: "What do I do now?"

Having exhausted the avenues I thought would help me, and having no success in finding a resolution, I requested an Inter-Service

Transfer to the United States Navy. The response to my request was "Marines Don't Quit!"

I hope you are beginning to see how difficult it was to trust anyone.

Looking back, there are so many things that have become clearer to me. Again, that is only because I was finally able to recognize the reality of what I had suffered. It has been a long, long journey.

WHAT IS UP WITH ME?

Let's talk about my civilian employment history. I began having anger issues relative to respecting authority. After working at specific jobs for long periods of time I found myself just quitting. On occasion, I might give two weeks notice, but then I would leave before the effective date of my resignation. Or, I would just quit without giving notice. Believe it or not, my behavior was puzzling and disturbing to even me. I felt like I was losing control of my own emotions and it scared me. But where was I to turn? Who would hear me? What in the world was happening?

My last counseling session, which lasted over three hours, occurred in 2013. I'm not certain what I was feeling, other than anger, once the session concluded.

The session began with the psychiatrist asking me: "do you know why you are here?" I responded by saying I was there to prove that I was not, am not, a liar. He, of course, took objection to how I was viewing this matter. Did you catch that? Once again, I am in a room with a man I don't know, with the door closed. How much sense does any of this make? But the session began.

Psychiatrist: Tell me about your childhood.

How many times have we visited that question? More importantly, has anybody listened to my consistent response? Having to start back at square one again did not make me a happy person.

To give you some perspective: at the time of this session, I was in the fourth year of my claim review. And, on his desk was a copy of my file. It measured approximately ten inches deep. Not long into the session, his questions caused me to ask him: "have you read this?" He stated he had as he slapped the file with his hand. I was surprised to see dust fly. He told me: it seems your claim was placed in a corner and forgotten.

Oh, goodie!

Yes, many of us have read or heard about the VA backlog. Well, I am here to tell you it is real. I don't care what anybody says. The VA backlog is very real.

Back to our session. Once we got past the fact that my family was not to blame for what was going on with me, he stated: "You are angry aren't you?"

"Yes, I am."

"And you have been angry for a long period of time haven't you?"

"Yes, I have."

I didn't say this to him but I was thinking: "Who in the hell wouldn't be? Forty-two years is a long time to have dealt with the effects of Military Sexual Trauma.

Needless to say, the professionals have a format they must follow to ensure fairness to all when dealing with this issue. My disappointment at not being able to interject at various times became very frustrating. For instance: I tried to point out that people of a higher rank than your own have all the power. That in the military, rank and the chain of command are the "be all and end all." He interrupted me to announce that what I said meant "nothing to him as he was not a Veteran and didn't understand the rank structure."

Are you for real? You, the doctor, who is working for a veterans organization, don't understand the importance of rank within the structure?

Well, let me tell you: it is everything. Be it good or bad, if you have the rank, you have the power.

As you can imagine we covered a great deal of territory within the time frame allotted. Some of the questions made sense or, at least, seemed to make sense. Others I found to be insulting, embarrassing, accusatory, and sadly comical. And I don't mean in an entertaining fashion.

Looking back at the experience, I suppose he was trying to determine a number of things: my mental stability, sincerity, level of comfort, etcetera. To be blunt, all I wanted was to get away from him. I was extremely uncomfortable being in a one-on-one environment with him. Matter of fact, I asked him to open the door to his office during this session, and also asked that a female be present.

He opened the door but explained he could not provide a female for at least another two weeks. Yep, so here I am, four years into this and I might be looking at another two weeks.

I don't think so!

I could not give this another minute. I could not take any more questions, not one more. I just wanted to leave. I wanted to get away from him and from this entire matter. I wanted to hide somewhere. I wanted to cry. I wanted to sleep. I wanted to disappear. I wanted to understand what was happening but I couldn't find an answer. My emotions were jumbled and all I could hear was my heartbeat. Where was my safe place?

It was not yet found. I had not yet finished this wearisome and ugly journey.

I believe the doctor sensed my anxiety. I imagine he also knew that, despite my debilitating emotions, I was determined to continue the process of my claim. There would be no quitting!

TRIGGERS

The most difficult and painful experience of this entire journey was having to identify triggers. These were the things affecting my behavior in a negative way. What triggers caused me to flashback to the traumatic experience that was the genesis of my trauma and my emotional suffering? In my experience, it was several things. Some make sense but others do not. Regardless, the intensity of the trigger-moment is terrifying.

Okay, what say we identify some triggers?

Having been attacked from behind, I am extremely careful not to expose my back to a perceived danger.

I do not sit with my back to a door. If I must, e.g. at church, I am extremely uncomfortable. Not at restaurants, staff meetings, private dinner parties, etcetera. I can't tell you the last time I have been to a movie. It is impossible to not sit with your back to the door at a movie. Even at outdoor events I am careful not to turn my back to the crowd. You got it! My life has been controlled by many limitations as a result of being assaulted.

Unless I can identify more than one escape from a room, I do not enter.

Loud noises are extremely upsetting for various and probably obvious reasons. Being attacked is not a quiet event. Grunting, groaning, heavy breathing, the shifting of furniture, and being slammed against a wall result in a myriad of noises.

Driving in heavy traffic is an event I try to avoid. Panic sets in when I am surrounded on all sides by rapid movement. Once again, being attacked is not a slow-paced event. At some point during the attack, balance, focus, and logic seem to be out of reach and time seems to go on forever.

The smell of an abscessed tooth brings me to a stand-still. I find it difficult to breath and become fearful of my surroundings.

Note: when I mentioned the abscessed tooth to the doctor he was dismissive of the importance. He stated: "Well how often does that happen?" Got news for you, Doc — more than you know. A great many people do not practice good oral hygiene. And yes, that included my attacker.

The sound of heavy breathing or panting is definitely a trigger for some intense emotional flash backs.

For instance: all animals pant or breath heavily at times. Even babies can have their own rhythm of breathing or panting. At any rate, he again said: "Well how often does that happen?" I explained to him that I go to the gym five days a week and there is a tremendous amount of heavy breathing going on there. He looked shocked and said: "Why do you do that? It makes no sense."

Here it is again, Doc. As a result of my falling down a flight of stairs and suffering an injury as a result of that fall, The VA hospital recommended I work out at the gym to provide greater mobility, and to ease the pain. Weight lifters, bodybuilders, swimmers, cyclists, joggers, and marathoners do a great deal of heavy breathing. "What do you think, Doc?" My being at the gym is a must to improve my comfort level. It is not an elective pastime.

While I could go on providing "triggers" I don't believe it is necessary. You get the point.

Suffice it to say, any of your senses may react to something and cause a flashback. Just so you know.

Michelle F. Capucci

ARE WE DONE?

So now the doctor and I have spent three hours together and I am exhausted, angry, suspicious, and look forward to leaving his office.

Finally, the doctor stands up, heads to the door and comes to a stop with his back resting against the door frame, halfway in the room and halfway out. I don't know if he knew how intimidating that was for me but if he did, shame on him. He reached toward me (oh my God) to shake my hand and said: "Thank you for your service." Once I was able to compose myself (not that he noticed) we spoke briefly of attitudes during the Vietnam Conflict. Honestly, at that point, I could not recall ever being thanked for my service to this

222

country.

Leaving his office felt to me like *The Great Escape*. I wanted to throw up just to rid myself of all I'd just been reminded of during the session: the pain, anxiety, panic, fear, suspicion, and distrust. I wanted to vomit this ugly event out of my system. I will compare it to eating spoiled food. You know if you can bring yourself to vomit you will feel better. Sadly, I was not dealing with spoiled food. So there I was stuck with the ugliness of it all. I left his office wondering: Are we done? Is this it? Should I continue looking for a safe place? What now?

DON'T MISUNDERSTAND QUITTING

Upon arriving home I just could not identify what I was feeling. I felt exhausted. I felt numb. I felt out of touch with everything.

What did I do at this point? I quit! I gave up! But not in the way you may be thinking. My decision to quit encompassed my emotional well-being only. I had come too far to totally call it quits. I had to find a safe place and the only way I could do that was to listen to my inner self. It was telling me to give my emotions a break. It was telling me to seek R&R to enable me to finish this forced march. In other words, don't misunderstand quitting. In this case it's more like pausing. Take my word: escaping for short periods of time are pretty healthy and definitely necessary.

After a few days, I contacted my navigator and we chatted about various things. She could hear the hurt and distrust in my voice.

Let me say this to you again, reader: if you find yourself walking this path you are going to want to quit. Don't do it! Did you hear me? And if you have a navigator and they are doing their job, they will encourage you to stay the course. Do not quit! Take a break, but do not quit!

Did you hear me?

AT LONG LAST

Are you sitting down? Well, please do.

Here we are five years later and my claim regarding Military Sexual Trauma has been approved and found to be "compensable." What does that mean to me? Very simply, it means I am validated at last! It means somebody was listening! It means I no longer have to prove I am not, was not a liar.

It also means more.

I had hidden this terrible event for many, many years. But what I found in reliving it all was the following: The truth shall set you free. No more hiding, no more excuses, and no more fooling myself. When you can say to yourself: I am a victim of Military Sexual

Assault, you will know freedom. Accepting the fact you are a victim is liberating.

Now all we have to do is **find a** way to move beyond this mess and surround ourselves with **nothing** but positive energy.

FORGIVE AND FORGET

It would be nice to think the ol' forgive and forget philosophy would work in this situation. Honestly, don't kid yourself into thinking moving ahead is a piece of cake. It is anything but. Stop right now and think of all the people you might consider forgiving under these circumstances. Notice, I used the word consider. Beyond the facet of forgiveness, are we truly expected to forget this journey from hell? I don't think so.

Maybe some scenarios in life allow more room for reaching the forget level. But I do not believe sexual assault is one of them. Personally, I don't want to forget. I want to remain vigilant when it comes to my surroundings. I want to listen to my gut instincts when it comes to trusting people, or not, and I want to recognize anything out of the ordinary. No, I would not be able to achieve this if I elected to forget.

Forgiveness is more a matter of our own well-being rather than for those to whom we present the gift: the gift of forgiveness. We must be good to ourselves before we can be good to others.

I am not certain I can round up all the bad guys I might consider forgiving. Without a doubt I must place my attacker at the top of my list. Talk about a challenge! For me to forgive this person I must tap the depths of my very soul. Was I strong enough to forgive my attacker? Yes! But that was for my benefit. If you hang on to all this negativity you are allowing someone or some thing to continue beating you up.

Did I miss out on various phases of my life as a result of this attack? Yes. I shared with you earlier that I wondered what I may have achieved had I not experienced this horrible event. Doubting my ability to make the right choices in everyday life was at times terrifying.

Mostly, I wondered how my inability to trust affected

potential relationships, employment opportunities, and friendships. Not being a mind reader left me always questioning the motives of others. I was not capable of trusting. Why is this so significant?

Trust, as I see it, is earned. There is no substitute for sitting down with a trusted friend, co-worker, or family member and sharing your pain, fears, or insecurities. But when the exposure of vulnerability or weakness is met with: "That's in the past, get over it;" it is an extreme shock and disappointment. Needless to say, those who should have been there for me let me down. All I was saying to them was: I don't expect you to totally understand what I am talking about, but I'd hoped you were listening. Did you hear me?

Not considering myself to be a controlling individual, I welcome many different thoughts and ideas. But when my integrity is questioned it brings consequences. Let me repeat. You may question my integrity but it has consequences. Believing a person comes into this world with nothing I also believe that the only thing we leave behind is our reputation. When a friend questioned my integrity it led to the loss of that friend.

Losing a friend on this journey was unexpected but

inevitable, I suppose. Did you know that people tend to believe a lie over the truth? I've come to accept this. I cannot change human nature. What I can do is try to understand the root cause of such silliness. I choose to blame this former friend's position on naivety. I choose to blame it on this friend's inability to step outside their comfort zone. Can I forgive that? Yes. Do I want to extend my forgiveness to forgetting. No. I lost a friend. And I will not forget.

Keeping in mind that Military Sexual Assault is a well-kept secret, there are other actors in this matter who I must consider forgiving. Who are they?

This is really rich! I had to consider forgiving my Priest. Yes, you heard me. Father X was one of the people to whom I went seeking advice and guidance in the very beginning. In a round-a-bout way he gave me that. It just wasn't what I expected.

"Pursuing this matter will ruin your career and will jeopardize your security clearance" he'd said. Well, there you have it. There was my limited advice and guidance. And yes, while he may have been straightforward with me, I did not feel comforted. In those days, comfort was elusive. I thought about this priest and about how I'd felt abandoned. I thought long and hard, and in the end, I forgave him.

Let's move on to those who were my military bosses when the assault occurred. As I asserted before: people often believe lies over the truth. And if you haven't learned that yet, pay attention.

As horrible as it sounds, some people seem unable to differentiate between sex and sexual assault. Saying "It's human nature" is a terrible way to respond to someone who has suffered this kind of traumatic event. As you may have guessed, I was dealing with all men at the office. I knew no matter what I said it would not be accepted as truth. Can I forget that? Not at this moment. Can I forgive? Yes.

Eventually I was transferred to another assignment within the Marine Corps. It consisted of an all female compliment. In fairness, I must tell you that the ladies I worked for have my utmost respect to this day. I am speaking about respect as it relates to their knowledge, skills, and ability to lead and command.

Yet, here we are in the late 1960's dealing with a complaint regarding Military Sexual Trauma. What did my female superiors do?

Made like ostriches sticking their heads in the sand hoping it would all go away. As I have stated, there were no guidelines for processing a complaint of this nature. Even though logic told us something was systemically wrong we had no compass. Can I forget the realness of those times? No! What would be the point of looking at history if we were just to forget it?

This was when I requested that inter-service transfer to the United States Navy. Silly me, I didn't give consideration to the reality that Military Sexual Trauma (MST) existed in all branches of the armed services. Why would I even have to consider that reality? Jeez, I was young and unschooled in the ways of the world! My request for a transfer was met with: "Marines Don't Quit."

There you have it. I knew no other avenue to pursue that would offer safety. Why do I say that? The physical attack was over but the on-going attempts at character assassination seemed non-stop. Have I forgiven the "Marines Don't Quit" solution? No.

Obviously, there were people I encountered along the way that I cannot forgive. Now don't get me wrong. I don't dwell on the negative. And yes, I know for my own benefit I should reconsider forgiveness for these people. Maybe one day.

Not forgiving works against me because negative energy is a killer and it allows the unforgiven to win the battle. What goes around comes around is comforting to consider. I am a big believer in Karma. Yet, I don't feel consumed with negative energy as a result of not forgiving those I cannot forgive. It's just the way it is.

Am I being overly critical or sensitive about this. No way. You see, my response to this subject of forgive and forget made me realize I was on the mend. I was going to become me.

Whoever that is.

WHO AM I TODAY?

You would think that after forty-two years of dealing with this matter, the answer would be evident or obvious. But it is not.

Let me try again.

I don't feel the need to categorize myself. We humans are an odd breed. It seems everything has to be defined relative to our being. Well, I choose to believe my being is constantly evolving. Therefore, assigning a category would be a waste of precious time.

Like you I have valuable skills, talents, dreams, wishes, hopes, and fears. I am, above all, a good listener. You don't have to ask me: "Did you hear me?" I not only heard you, I truly listened to what you had to say.

I offer advice when I feel it is appropriate and if I feel it will be received in the manner intended. It can be slippery, though, so I am cautious. Be warned: the lack of trust in most people leads them to believe you may have a hidden agenda just because you are kind to them. The realization is you cannot sway their opinions. In these cases, the best thing to do is offer support when asked.

When able, I am a generous person. No, I am not talking about giving lavishly. I am talking about paying for someone's groceries when I can. Giving of my time is especially fun. Volunteering is my favorite thing to do and is especially rewarding when addressing at-risk-youth. And if you have not noticed our youth are at risk. Look around you and if possible get involved. Be a mentor or a genuine friend.

And yes, I am still a victim of Military Sexual Trauma. And with a pang in my heart, I now know it will always be a part of who I am today, and today is all we have.

I am a person with a diagnosis of PTS, Post Traumatic Stress, and I have intentionally omitted the word "disorder." As I have said to many others, Post Traumatic Stress is not a disorder. It is an injury requiring treatment. Does this diagnosis mean I am going to explode at any moment? No, it means I finally know what I have been dealing with for most of my adult life.

And if you know of others who suffer from PTS, please be very hesitant to place judgment, as they too have suffered an injury in some form or another. If they trust you enough to share their pain, be a good listener and offer your unbridled support when it is appropriate.

Who am I today? I truly don't know and that is fine with me. I am a person continuing to evolve into whatever it is I was meant to be.

I am a gentle soul and so I try to protect myself from negative energy. In my opinion, positive energy is the key to survival.

To continue: when I am feeling lost and alone or troubled by the day's events, I return to the only things that comfort me. The memories of my childhood and music, music, music.

Please don't feel that I am insisting you turn to music for your comfort. I am, however, suggesting you turn to whatever it is that makes you feel safe. It may be a walk along the shore, a hike in the mountains, or just lying down in the tall grass watching the birds fly. Mother nature can provide inner peace. Give it a try.

When I realized my strength was found in solitude it was a wonderful awakening. I began to know myself. It takes work to discover who we really are, but it is well worth the energy expended.

Try this: picture yourself sitting before an easel and facing a blank canvas. With brushes in hand you anticipate the creative energy soon to flow from your being. Now, without any preconceived idea as to what you would like to put on the canvas, just dip the brush in the paint. It doesn't matter what color or how much you apply, just make contact with the canvas and simply let the brush do the work. Give the brush that represents you free reign and watch what happens.

Are you disappointed there is not a Rembrandt staring back at you? I hope not.

Step back from your work and look at what you have created. Is it a reflection of your inner-being? If not, look deep inside and grab another brush. Your work is not complete. Keep in mind you are not trying to become anyone else but you. You are not meant to copy anybody else's work. This is about your freedom to express all kinds of things crying out for release: happiness, sadness, joy, pain, sunny days, rainy days, and all the seasons of our lives.

Why are there so many colors from which to choose? Because you are a complex and beautiful person requiring an array of colors to define your character. Don't hesitate to dabble in the colors that draw the attention of your brush.

In case you are wondering, I have gone through countless numbers of brushes, canvasses, and colors of paint while creating my own masterpiece. What I discovered was this: everything takes time and patience. I have learned that you must not try to control the brush if you truly want to display and appreciate your inner-self. To coin a phrase: take a deep breath, relax, and go with the flow.

In case you haven't noticed, I learned the following about myself: Mother Nature, music, and art fill me with a deep sense of serenity while at the same time, providing strength. And if I am meant to be a loner, so be it. At the very least it provides the quiet moments I have known and enjoyed: the first snowfall of winter or an electric sunset at the end of summer.

As you well know, life is a complicated journey. Even so, there are a few narratives out there that seem to express what we need to find inner peace, writings that help us understand ourselves and the universe. Many years ago I found just such a narrative. It addresses many of my questions, causes me to reflect, and gives me new direction each time I read it. The poem is *Desiderata* by Max Ehrmann:

Go placidly amid the noise and the haste, and remember what peace there may be in silence. As far as possible, without surrender, be on good terms with all persons.

Speak your truth quietly and clearly; and listen to others, even to the dull and the ignorant; they too have their story.

Avoid loud and aggressive persons; they are vexatious to the spirit. If you compare yourself with others, you may become vain or bitter, for always there will be greater and lesser persons than yourself.

Enjoy your achievements as well as your plans. Keep interested in your own career, however humble; it is a real possession in the changing fortunes of time.

Exercise caution in your business affairs, for the world is full of trickery.

But let this not blind you to what virtue there is; many persons strive for high ideals, and everywhere life is full of heroism.

Be yourself. Especially, do not feign affection. Neither be cynical about love; for in the face of all aridity and disenchantment, it is as perennial as the grass.

Take kindly the counsel of the years, gracefully surrendering the things of youth.

Nurture strength of spirit to shield you in sudden misfortune. But do not distress yourself with dark imaginings. Many fears are born of fatigue and loneliness.

Beyond a wholesome discipline, be gentle with yourself. You are a child of the universe no less than the trees and the stars; you have a right to be here.

And whether or not it is clear to you, no doubt the universe is unfolding as it should. Therefore be at peace with God, whatever you conceive Him to be.

And whatever your labors and aspirations, in the noisy confusion of life, keep peace in your soul. With all its sham, drudgery and broken dreams, it is still a beautiful world. Be cheerful. Strive to be happy.

The bottom line: you must believe you are not alone, you must do what is best for you. You must find a good way to ease your pain and suffering.

Did you hear me?

Believe me when I tell you: if I can survive this, so can you.

IS IT OVER?

My parents did a great job in raising me. I called upon the lessons they taught me many times while evaluating my worth. Do I like me? Yes! And I am beginning to see more and more of the goodness that was almost destroyed by a violent act 42 years ago.

I have never been a POW, but I can imagine the day-to-day struggle just to focus on what is real. Being comfortable in your own skin does not offer a timeline for how to achieve this level of comfort. So I cannot offer you a precise formula for reaching this goal. But I can suggest you stay strong and surround yourself with positive people and energy. Listen to yourself, follow your heart and believe in no other being but you.

Did you hear me?

Now what should you do about you? I can't know for certain but I will suggest the following. If you need a navigator to help you through this horrible maze of doubt, criticism, name calling, hissing, finger pointing, unfounded accusations, government forms, and various levels of the VA bureaucracy, then give yourself a gift and find that navigator. Contact your local veterans organization and let them help you carry the load. Seek professional help when you feel you are in crisis. Even though we like to view ourselves as being strong there are times when we cannot walk alone.

Do what you believe in your heart to be best for you. And when that happens we can look forward to halting this forced march, remove our full gear, unpack our sea bags, and embrace a good night's sleep.

ACKNOWLEDGMENTS

To my friends and respected acquaintances: I must say you have been there for me from the beginning. Your faith and constant support has driven me to cross the finish line regarding the topic of Military Sexual Trauma. Thank you for your patience, trust, and kindness – without which this would not have been possible.

Wendell Ward, you are not only a very talented editor, but a man of character. Thank you for your devotion and belief in the goodness of my work. You have renewed my faith in trusting once again. And anyone who reads this book will come to understand how very important being able to trust again is to me. You are the best, my friend.

Cover design by Daniel J. H. McDonald

ABOUT THE AUTHOR

Michelle F. Capucci was raised in an environment that promoted and encouraged respect for others; one in which steadfast integrity was of paramount importance. These characteristics served her well in her chosen career working in the field of human resources and volunteering with youth at risk. She is a lifetime member of the Women Marines Association, and continues to show pride in her service to this nation.

Visit Michelle at: michelle.capucci@yahoo.com

Made in United States
Troutdale, OR
12/09/2023